Church and State in Medieval Europe 1050–1314

Church and State in Medieval Europe 1050-1314

Thomas J. Renna

Saginaw Valley College

Cover design by Sherry Enrico.

From Giotto's Dream of Innocent III: a beggar holds up the crumbling church.

KENDALL/HUNT PUBLISHING COMPANY
DUBUQUE, IOWA

for
Pamela S. Renna

Contents

Preface

This book is an introduction to the study of medieval Europe. Rather than attempt to scan a large number of names and events, I limit this guide to a few select problems, or test cases, concerning France, Germany, and Italy during the period 1050-1314. My purpose is to erect a rhetorical model which will portray some of the era's major political, institutional, cultural, and religious developments. By this glance at the middle ages I hope to get the reader to share my enthusiasm for a period when many of our modern ways of thinking and acting were nurtured. If my reader afterwards discards this book and seeks out more information on matters medieval, I shall be gratified.

Professor George D. Balsama of Kent State University suggested that I write this book. I deeply appreciate his encouragement and concern throughout. My gratitude extends to my former advisor, Professor William M. Bowsky of the University of California at Davis, and to Professor Sylvia Thrupp of the University of Michigan at Ann Arbor who both kindly offered useful advice on the MS. I am thankful for the incisive remarks on language style by Dean Curtis McCray of Saginaw Valley College and by Professor Jane Eberwein of Oakland University. My former mentor, Professor Bryce Lyon of Brown University, made helpful suggestions on the entire MS. In this as in previous scholarly projects Professor Lyon has been ever present with his support and wise counsel. His witness to historical scholarship has been an inspiration to me.

A special debt of gratitude goes to Carolyn Davis, Reference Librarian at Saginaw Valley College, whose persistence put the interlibrary loan system to its most severe test as a result of her quest for obscure journals. The sure hand of Sherry Enrico designed the attractive cover. I have immensely enjoyed and profited from conversations on medieval history with my students at Saginaw Valley College both in and out of class. Finally, my most relentless critic was my wife, Pamela, to whom this book is dedicated. Out of our endless discussions on each of the many revisions of this book emerged the pages which follow.

Introduction

The political, institutional, and cultural life of medieval civilization is clearly revealed in the era's relations between church and state. These relations can be concretely observed through the lives of five pairs of personalities: Pope Gregory VII and Emperor Henry IV, St Bernard of Clairvaux and Abelard, St Francis of Assisi and Pope Innocent III, Emperor Frederick II and King Louis IX of France, King Philip the Fair and Pope Boniface VIII. These ten men reflect in microcosm certain church-state problems in Europe during the high middle ages.

The period 1050-1314 begins and ends with a revolution. The first was started by a pope who had a dream of an organized European community. The second revolution was directed by a king who created the antithesis of the papal hope: the national state. The first hope was dying by 1314; the second is still alive but not well in the West of 1973.

Some warnings are needed for the student first encountering his or her medieval past. Modern novels and Hollywood movies notwithstanding, the actual power of kings and popes over the minds and behavior of medieval people was severely limited. Centralized, bureaucratic governments were just beginning to emerge. Before the thirteenth century people expected little from government, and they got little. Anything more forceful than settling a fight was called tyranny.

While this book examines popes working for universal order, it must not be imagined that this order actually existed. Europe from 1000 to 1300 became increasingly prosperous economically, but it was politically and socially unstable. Conditions in medieval Europe varied greatly from region to region and century to century.

Modern Americans tend to conceive of the middle ages as an age of faith, a time when religion supposedly reigned supreme. Perhaps this myth about the period persists because it accords with modern man's smug notions about progress. The previous era must have been superstitious and primitive, it is intuited, because the present era is allegedly scientific and civilized. At any rate, there were probably as many atheists in the twelfth century as there are in the twentieth. Surviving twelfth-century documents often reflect a religious bias since most literate people were priests.

The "conflict" between church and state was for the most part mild and mutually productive. The conflict rarely involved questions of principle. Rather, the issues were largely those of disputed legal boundaries, e.g., the precise extent of a king's right to tax a particular town. Something like the Congress-President dualism in the United States, the church-state dichotomy functioned as a sort of check and balance system, with each side prodding the other to ever greater social utility. The vehement anticlerical and antipapal sentiments expressed by some emperors were relatively uncommon before the fourteenth century.

In twentieth-century America, church-state clashes involve such peripheral problems as parochiaid and prayer in the schools. In twelfth-century Europe, church-state battles were tips of icebergs, the surface manifestations of currents deep within society. The manner in which a person reacted to such conflicts mirrored his most basic values regarding himself, his community, his deity.

The drama of medieval Europe is a tragedy, a very human tragedy. A group of men tried to realize the lofty hope of a giant commonwealth united in Christian love. But the goal proved elusive. The means which were invented to attain this end themselves became goals. When the idealism passed, society was left with an albatross of its own making.

That the Roman Pontiff alone is rightly to be called universal.

Gregory VII

I _____

THE FIRST REVOLUTION: POPE GREGORY VII AND EMPEROR HENRY IV

The church and the state in Europe were born during the Investiture Conflict (1050-1122). At this time men could conceptualize a unified, autonomous church and also a state with its own power. Prior to 1050 the lines between church and state were blurred beyond recognition. After this date the higher clergy more often referred to itself as a church within Christian society. Many clerics believed that God had called them to shape and direct society according to biblical principles. This community of priests and laymen was called Christendom.

So too the state emerged as a distinct power. A few rulers, in particular the Holy Roman Emperor, had minds broad enough to imagine something like a Christendom. The state's special role within this supersociety was to protect the lives, property, and rights of its members. The state was supposed to take care of the physical and temporal needs; the clerical church, the spiritual.

Most men and women in 1050 were not aware of a "Christendom," nor did such a monster seem desirable. Their parochial views hardly extended over the next hill. These people became uncomfortable at the thought of an army of priestly leaders or the goose step of knights from the royal palace. At most, they had some hazy notion that they, as "Christians," were somehow different from faraway "infidels" (Muslims, Vikings, Magyars).

Tension between church and state became evident with the appearance of two strong men, each of whom insisted that he and he alone was supposed to command the church universal. While the clash between Pope Gregory VII (1073-85) and Holy Roman Emperor Henry IV (1056-1106) was no doubt exacerbated by their incompatible personalities, it was also an attempt to settle the issue of who should rule in Italy and Germany. The answer to this question would decide the course of European history and affect the daily life of even the most obscure peasant. Before the larger-than-life figures of Henry and Gregory are treated, the situation in Italy and Germany must be grasped.

ITALY AROUND 1050

In Italy political and ecclesiastical conditions were in flux. "Italy" was a mere geographical term of convenience, for even the larger territories of Lombardy,

Tuscany, Spoleto, Sicily, and the Papal States had their
share of internal disputes and conflicting claims to jurisdiction. The great manufacturing and trading cities of
Lombardy were especially unstable due to economic
rivalries and to internal class wars. The emperor always
considered Italy a rightful part of his empire. To subdue
rebellious nobles in Germany, he needed the wealth of
the Lombard cities and the moral support of the Lombard reformers and the papacy.

When Emperor Henry III, an advocate of church reform, appointed Leo IX (1049-54) to the holy see, a
new chapter in European history began. While Leo IX
had no intention of opposing his near relative Henry III,
he steered the papacy on an independent course. Too
often in the past the papacy was a puppet manipulated
by the emperor or the great noble families in Rome. The
papacy, an office which was attached to vast tracts of
land, had long been a prize for ambitious Roman families. Caught in this cross fire the pope played little role
in the reform movements which emanated mainly from
Lorraine, Cluny, and Lombardy. But Leo IX, who filled
papal offices with his German friends, was determined
to liberate the see of St Peter from the mire of Roman
politics, and to "restore" to that see the position of
moral supremacy in the church universal. This romantic
view of the papacy was brought in from northern
Europe, since it was there that the Irish and English
missionaries of Carolingian times fired up enthusiasm
for a kind of vague spiritual guidance from the Apostle
of Rome.

Fortunately for the papalist reformers who infiltrated
Rome after Leo IX, Henry IV (1056-1106), the son of
Henry III, was five years old at his father's death. As is
common in monarchies governed by a minor, a series of
power struggles revolved around the tutelage of the
young king. These squabbles among rival princely families kept the Germans preoccupied with affairs north of

the Alps. This breathing space permitted the reformist popes to consolidate the Papal States in central Italy and fight the Roman nobles for control of papal elections. Leo IX's successors, inspired by his example, scurried around Italy and Europe sanctioning reform and cementing alliances with ecclesiastics and secular princes. These popes championed the elimination of simony (buying church offices), clerical marriages (married bishops and abbots tended to be solicitors of the aristocratic families of which they were part), violence against church lands by rapacious nobles, and moral corruption within the priesthood. They seized opportunities to arbitrate disputes and, by so doing, created precedents for a uniform legal code which would apply only to priests. Canon law would prove to be the most potent weapon in the construction of the papal monarchy.

Pope Nicholas II (1059-61) formalized two dreams of the reformers. He issued the famous Electoral Decree which lifted the power to elect a pope out of the hands of the turbulent Roman aristocracy, and placed it in the hands of the cardinals, or papal advisors. Henceforth the pope must be chosen by the college of cardinals (from one of their number) and ratified by the rest of the clergy and the important laymen of Rome. Moreover, the emperor was to voice his approval of the cardinals' choice. Thus the election of popes, at least on paper, was freed from lay interference, whether from the emperor or the Roman families. In addition to the Election Decree Nicholas II obtained from the Normans in Sicily the military assistance needed to put teeth into the Decree. In a surprisingly bold, almost cynical, "peace" treaty the pope parceled out territories in southern Italy and Sicily which in fact belonged to the Byzantine Emperor and the Muslims. In exchange for feudal overlordship (two Norman princes took an oath of fealty to Nicholas) and standby military aid, the pope gave plundering Norman leaders their long-desired legitimacy.

Nicholas II's diplomatic flip-flop illustrates the papacy's determination to operate as a free agent. By this desperate gamble the pope substituted the traditional protection of the emperor for the protection of the wily Normans. The papal-Norman alliance was but another insult the pope hurled at the Byzantine rulers. In 1054 the pope had precipitated a schism between the Eastern and Western churches by demanding Byzantine submission to the bishop of Rome.

The reform movement in Rome, as with all reform movements, had its radical fringe. The extreme left wing of the papalist party was dominated by Cardinal Humbert and Hildebrand, both of whom decried lay investiture and simony as "heresies." Lay investiture was the practice whereby the emperor bestowed the spiritual and temporal offices upon a newly elected bishop. Technically he was elected by the local cathedral canons, although in practice the choice of the candidate was influenced by the emperor. Since the emperor was the feudal overlord of the possessions which were attached to a bishopric, he had the right to receive homage from the newly selected lord of these lands. (Bishops and abbots were usually drawn from powerful noble families). Thus the bishop, just like any other vassal, became the vassal of the emperor. Because of this dual office—pastor of souls and the political head of large estates—the bishop was a leader in both church and state. But what, asked the radicals, gave the emperor the right to bestow the spiritual authority upon the new bishop? Is not the emperor, or any other secular ruler, a layman despite his exalted status? The emperor replied that he was not a mere layman but rather the divinely appointed defender of the faith. He was "king and priest," the successor of Constantine and Charlemagne. This theocratic concept of kingship, "by the grace of God," was accepted by virtually everyone in the eleventh century—everyone that is except Humbert and Hildebrand.

While most Christians, including clerics, saw no conflict of interest in the bishop's status as the spiritual
shepherd of his flock and also as the temporal lord of
the estates of his bishopric, ultrapapalists blasted lay
investiture as the root of all evil in Christian society. To
them, the emperor, or any other lay prince of this
world, had no business conferring episcopal powers on
anyone. Only churchmen had such powers. When the
emperor handed over the spiritual authority (symbolized by a staff) and the temporal power (symbolized by
a ring), the recipient had unlawfully "purchased" an
apostolic office. Therefore, argued Humbert, all priests
consecrated by this make-believe bishop were invalidly
ordained! If Humbert's demands were accepted, Europe
would have been turned on its head since most bishoprics and abbeys were tinged with simony. Humbert and
the extreme papalists wanted to free the church hierarchy from all lay control and place it under the control
of the papacy. By this simplistic yet compelling logic
the papalists insisted that their proposal was the panacea
which would restore order and true religion in the
church.

The day of the radical reformers arrived when one of
their own was uncanonically raised to the holy see.
Hildebrand, sometimes referred to as "Holy Satan," had
been around Rome since the time of Leo IX, and had
risen through the ranks quickly: subdeacon, cardinal,
papal legate, archdeacon. Hildebrand's reputation for
tough-minded fairness earned him respect among many
Roman factions. When a Roman mob carried Hildebrand to the papal throne the factions felt that a respite
of order might benefit the City.

GERMANY AROUND 1050

The situation in Germany was equally unstable. At
Henry III's death in 1056 the weakest struts in the
imperial umbrella strained near the breaking point. The

great princes, who painfully watched their independence ebb, resumed their usual diplomatic and military maneuvering in order to keep the emperor off balance. What made armed rebellion usually so ineffective were their own mutual jealousies and the emperor's ability to win support of bishops, abbots, petty nobles, and towns within the princes' territories. These disaffected groups within a principality were not enthusiastic monarchists; rather, their goal was to obtain relative freedom from the suffocating presence of the local prince. To add to the confusion, bishops and abbots wrangled with each other over landrights and tithes, a lucrative source of revenue. Finally, not all bishops were subservient to the crown, for some were affected by the reformist climate particularly in western Germany. A few were brave enough to condemn clerical marriage, simony, and even the emperor's interference in ecclesiastical affairs. These few expected pope and emperor to cooperate in the cause of reform.

When Henry IV declared himself of age at seventeen (1066), he had his hands full. He managed to pacify the princes by alternating promises with suppression. Henry came to realize, however, how dependent his realm was on the monasteries and the bishoprics. At all costs these church lands must fall under the emperor's purview if the rebellious princes were to be checked. No doubt the pope, his traditional ally, would assist him in this political task. But dissent continued in two areas: Saxony and northern Italy.

The duchy of Saxony was unique within the empire. Proud of their ancient heritage, the Saxons considered themselves an oppressed minority. The "reforms" of Henry III sought to divest the independent-minded Saxon nobles, lay and priestly, of their rights, and to assimilate them into the imperial order. Only in Saxony were the great nobles united with the lesser nobles vis-à-vis imperial knights and bureaucrats. Henry IV had to

postpone his Italian plans and muster all his resources to
quell the rising in the North.

THE MILAN AFFAIR

The wealthy Lombard cities rarely knew a moment's
peace. Too suspicious of each other to make lasting alliances they were the tempting prey of popes, emperors,
various Italian nobles, and princes of southern Germany.
When Milan rose in revolt it was clear that Henry must
retain control of the city if he were to achieve imperial
hegemony in Italy. The archbishop of Milan possessed
more political and ecclesiastical power than anyone in
Italy except perhaps the pope. The revolt in 1056 was
led by the Patarini ("rag-pickers") which included merchants and artisans. These two social classes overlooked
their economic and social differences for the moment in
order to strip the Milanese nobles of their political stran-
glehold. The merchants and artisans had come to realize
that they could not influence the government's economic policies (prices, wages, credit, indirect and direct
taxes of all kinds, coinage) without some political clout.
To give their unlawful dissent a veneer of respectability
the Patarini joined forces with the local religious reformers. Together they attacked the loose-living, married Milanese clergy who commonly paid handsome
sums for their positions. Popular Patarini preachers
harangued the citizenry in the market places, and in-
veighed against the worldly "foreign" bishops who were
appointees of the emperor.

The other Lombard bishops, also frequently of the
German nobility, sided with the archbishop and the
nobles lest the popular rebellion serve as an example to
their own urban flocks. The regency government of
Henry IV may have committed a tactical error by helping the conservative Lombard bishops elect an antipope,
for by so doing the emperor appeared to be an enemy of
the reform. Unfortunately for Henry IV's reputation his

own Lombard bishops finally abandoned their antipope and came over to the true pope, Alexander II (1061-73). Alexander sent Hildebrand as his personal legate to Milan to find a peaceful solution to the internal upheavals. Hildebrand convinced his pontiff that the papacy should ally with the nonnoble Patarini since they were the champions of ecclesiastical reform. Pope Alexander and the Patarini party chose the young Atto as the archbishop of Milan in 1072. Emperor Henry replied to Alexander's unholy alliance by investing with staff and ring one Godfrey who was then consecrated archbishop by the suffragan bishops of Milan. Shortly before he died on 21 April 1073, Alexander excommunicated Henry's counsellors.

POPE GREGORY VII
AND EMPEROR HENRY IV

There matters stood when Hildebrand became Pope Gregory VII (1073-85). The testimonies of his acquaintances and his prolific correspondence establish that the new pontiff was absolutely self-assured. The artless Gregory had little patience for argument or give and take. Whenever anyone, friend or foe, questioned his commands he attributed such insubordination to weakness or malice. His mind was neither legalistic nor scholarly. He was a moralist who rarely hesitated to overturn tradition in the cause of right. When it was a case of carrying out God's will no obstruction must be allowed to interfere. His courage and persistence were frequently sufficient to cow a stronger adversary. In his own eyes he was not a revolutionary. He believed that as a humble servant of the Lord he was simply advocating the customary policies and dogma of the Catholic church. As with many idealists Gregory sometimes felt pangs of guilt when his program was not instantly successful in all parts of Christendom. Gregory could not see that the applications of his interpretations of church

history and doctrine—orthodox though they were—
threatened to sweep away Europe as he knew it.

Emperor Henry IV was a different sort. He lacked
Gregory's iron will and idealism. Due to an unusual
upbringing the boy Henry was too neurotic and unstable
to have the statesmanlike qualities needed for the im-
perialship. Impulsive and moody, he alternated between
emotional displays of confidence and desperate acts of
self-assertion born of his feelings of inferiority. Yet this
lad had enough energy and quick-wittedness to keep his
barons disunited. Although he could effectively suppress
sporadic revolts, his inability to think in long-range
terms prevented him from fully exploiting the sound
monarchical institutions invented by his ancestors.

Henry's mother Agnes never mastered the regency.
She carried the bewildered young king with her on her
endless diplomatic excursions within Germany. She
never seemed able to decide which nobles could best
keep together her son's empire. In 1062 the duke of
Bavaria kidnapped Henry and proclaimed himself the
king's tutor. This bit of bravado gave Agnes the excuse
to abandon the regency and flee to a nunnery. Unfortunately for the state, Agnes was not the stuff of some
of the great women rulers of the time, such as Countess
Matilda of Tuscany.

Having been a plaything in the hands of the princes
for so long, Henry always felt the emotional need to
prove himself a man. He hated single-minded ideologues
like Hildebrand whom he never understood. Although
personally pious, Henry dealt with ecclesiastical matters
in political terms and expected his opponents to respond to his attacks in a similar manner. To the end
Henry did not accurately gauge the depth of the genuine
desire for church reform, a desire which could be useful
to the pope. The burden of proof was with the emperor
to demonstrate that he could direct religious reform better than the bishop of Rome. In existence for barely a

century the Holy Roman Empire was still searching for
its reason for being.

Despite this personality clash between Gregory and
Henry neither prince saw any reason why cooperation
was not possible. After all, had not pope and emperor at
times governed the empire together? Were they not both
interested in the temporal and spiritual needs of Christians? From the imperial side, the pope was the handmaiden of the emperor who therefore had the right of
ultimate decision. The pope's job according to this view
was to use his moral authority to keep God's empire
united. The emperor admitted that the pope had spiritual obligations, never clearly defined by anyone at the
time, to Christians outside the Holy Roman Empire.
The pope's prayers, finally, had special weight in heaven. The emperor's task was to mind the temporal requirements of Christians, and, together with the pope,
to work for their spiritual betterment as well. The trivial
points of disagreement since the time of Leo IX could
surely be straightened out.

From the papal side, this imperial perspective was
correct—up to a point. To be sure the emperor was the
Lord's anointed and had the awesome responsibility of
protecting the lives and property of good Christians. But
for Gregory *Rome* and Rome alone was the spiritual
focus of the entire Christian world. Any ecclesiastical
authority a secular prince might possess came from God
through the pope. The emperor's chief function was to
use the "material sword" (as the papalists referred to
the power of coercion) for the protection of God's
faith, God's church, and God's ministers (par excellence
the pope). If the emperor abused his function and impiously blocked the church's move to weed out sin and
heresy, he must be pushed aside with all deliberate
speed.

Gregory lost no time in pursuing his ends. Almost
immediately Gregory issued decrees forbidding married

priests and nicolaites (priests who harbored concubines) to celebrate mass, and deposing all priests who used money to gain their office. Furthermore, anyone who accepted a bishopric or abbey from a layman was automatically excommunicated. The layman who performed the investiture was similarly expelled from the church. During the first two years of his pontificate, Gregory, consulting no one except his council in Rome, merely spelled out what the extreme papalists had been advocating for more than twenty years. Emperor Henry voiced no protest since he was preoccupied with a Saxon rebellion.

In March 1075 some bureaucrat placed the Dictate of the Pope in the papal register. This curious document is a series of statements rather than a formal decree. Some of these headings include:

> That the Roman pontiff alone can with right be called universal.
> That he alone can depose or reinstate bishops.
> That he alone may use the imperial insignia.
> That he himself may be judged by no one.
> That of the pope alone all princes shall kiss the feet.
> That the Roman church has never erred, nor shall ever err.
> That it may be permitted to him to depose emperors.
> That he may absolve subjects from their fealty to wicked men.

The last statement suggests that only the pope can declare an emperor "wicked." The pope's astounding claim that he can depose emperors made it plain that Gregory would stop at nothing in his plan to reorganize the church under the papacy.

What is even more amazing than the decree against lay investiture (with its anti-imperial implications) and the Dictate of the Pope, is the character of Gregory's voluminous correspondence during 1073-75. These personal letters are a series of commands to the powerful throughout Europe. Pope Gregory orders the barons of France to go to Spain (which, Gregory reminds them, actually belongs to the pope) and expel the blaspheming

Muslims (30 April 1073). Gregory tells Beatrice of Tuscany to withdraw her support from the Lombard bishops (24 June 1073). Gregory reprimands the archbishop of Reims for persecuting the monks of St Remi and threatens to excommunicate him if he refuses to stop (30 June 1073). If the Duke of Bohemia disobeys the directives of the papal legates sent from Rome, Gregory threatens to "destroy" the Duke (8 July 1073). Gregory promises the Count of Burgundy a "reward from St Peter and St Paul" if he will send troops to Italy to defend the Papal States (2 February 1074). Gregory tells the abbot of Cluny, the most powerful abbot in Christendom, to come to Rome immediately to discuss unmentioned matters (19 March 1074). Gregory informs King Solomon of Hungary that his kingdom is actually under the jurisdiction of the pope (28 October 1074). There is no recorded reply of Solomon to this papal letter but he surely must have felt that some court jester had gone too far in concocting such an obvious forgery.

In these letters Gregory reveals no hesitation, only firm resolution. He had neither an army nor a bureaucracy to assist him in carrying out his commands. Gregory had little more than a handful of legates and some diplomatic connections with reformers outside Rome. His chief weapon was the awesome prestige of the papal office. The papacy was revered not only because of its association with the ancient Roman Empire and with the Prince of the Apostles, but also because Rome was the main storehouse of holy relics. What shocked contemporaries about Gregory's actions was his propensity to interpret the papal power in *jurisdictional* terms. No pope had tried to abrogate the spiritual and temporal rights of emperors. Gregory behaved, it was said, as if only he could judge the qualifications of secular and ecclesiastical princes throughout the whole of Christendom.

Feeling confident over his decisive defeat of the
Saxons in 1075, Henry IV returned to the Milan question. During the same year the Milanese nobles regained
their political supremacy following the sudden death of
the Patarini leader. The nobles immediately asked Henry
IV to replace archbishop Atto, a papal protégé, with
their own candidate, Tebald. Henry was only too glad to
depose Atto and invest Tebald; he also invested two
other bishops of his choosing—within the borders of the
Papal States. Henry even attempted, unsuccessfully, to
regain his sphere of influence in southern Italy by allying with an excommunicated Norman leader. If Henry
had managed to cement this Sicilian alliance the pope's
enemies would have surrounded the Papal States. This
encirclement would have blocked Gregory's plans since
strong military and diplomatic ties were essential to
secure papal freedom of action. How could a pope
remove incompetent bishops, invariably backed by private economic interests and political factions, if he
lacked the means to carry out his orders?

Gregory replied to this breach of faith—Henry
promised in 1073 to uphold the pope's choice of Milan's
archbishop—with a harsh letter (8 December 1075)
scolding Henry for hampering the "freedom of the
church," one of Gregory's favorite phrases. Since when,
Gregory thunders in this letter, can laymen appoint
bishops? Everyone knows that only the pope—"To thee
[Peter] are given the keys of Heaven, and whatsoever
thou shalt loose on earth shall be loosed in Heaven"—
has the ultimate right to consecrate bishops. Even when
an archbishop consecrates a suffragan bishop, the latter,
if any doubt arises, must be judged worthy by the holy
pontiff. Apparently, Henry, you have been listening to
the Devil's counsels. If you do not immediately dismiss
these three so-called bishops you will have to be cut off
from the communion of the Holy Church like a dead
branch.

When this letter was read to the emperor he is reported to have turned blood red. Before he could calm himself he summoned two archbishops and 24 bishops to a synod where Gregory VII was solemnly declared deposed. The imperial letter, rubber-stamped by the German bishops, began: "Henry, King not by usurpation, but by pious ordination of God to Hildebrand, now not pope, but false monk," and ended: "I, Henry, King [Henry had not yet been crowned Emperor of the Romans by a pope] by the grace of God, together with all our bishops, say to you: Descend! Descend!" A pope, declares Henry in this letter, has no right to depose a king (except for heresy) whose power comes not from the pope but directly from God. The king is responsible to God alone. The fanatic Gregory, the letter continues, tramples on tradition and the teachings of the Scriptures by interfering with the election of bishops, and meddling in politics all over the empire. By these scandals Gregory, who far away in Rome had to rely on secondhand information, has stirred up dissention and destructive rivalry within the Body of Christ. Gregory's own election was uncanonical and therefore invalid; it also was the result of bribery and coercion. After this salvo by Henry no compromise was possible. The War of Investitures had begun.

When the letters of Henry and the German bishops were read to a Lenten synod then in session, Gregory barely managed to prevent the synod members from lynching the German messengers. While passions were still inflamed Gregory quickly drafted a sentence of excommunication *and* deposition. This unusual decree, which is in the form of a prayer to St Peter, begins by repeating the Petrine doctrine (the pope is the personal delegate of St Peter who had charge of all Christians). Gregory claims to act for the "defense of your [Peter's] church." By Peter's power:

I deprive King Henry ... who has rebelled against thy
church with unheard-of audacity, of the government over
the whole kingdom of Germany and Italy, and I release all
Christian men from the allegiance which they have sworn or
may swear to him, and I forbid anyone to serve him as king.

Only the pope could reinstate this excommunicate into
the bosom of the church.

CIVIL WAR IN GERMANY

Unexpectedly several German dukes, who feared the
emperor's increased power following his victory over the
Saxons, seized this opportunity to form a conspiracy.
The right of a vassal to rebel against his lord, who had
violated the feudal contract, was a time-honored custom. Far from declaring their "independence," the
dukes rebelled to regain their "rightful" (i.e., customary) jurisdiction over churches and towns within
their fiefs. A few of these German princes joined the
intrigue out of religious beliefs which included even the
spiritual supremacy of the pope. Many nobles, at best
nominally Christian, had a superstitious fear of ecclesiastical excommunication which was seen as a kind of
diabolical curse. But the majority of the disaffected
princes had no concern for Gregory's programs and certainly had no intention of being subservient to the holy
see. They would not supplant one tyrant with another.
Rather, they saw in the pope's excommunication of
Henry the legal sanction they needed to legitimize their
rebellion against the emperor. They sought to exploit
the pope's position as supreme spiritual lord. The nobles
did not see the pope in distant Rome as a threat to their
political power.

It is clear that Henry made a mistake in challenging
Gregory so tactlessly in the Milan incident and in "ex-
communicating" him. Henry underestimated Gregory's
latent support and the depth of the discontent among
the German nobility. The imperial tax collectors and

judges had irritated so many people that even lesser nobles joined their overlords in the rebellion. Only the majority of the bishops who owed their status to the emperor were fairly consistent in siding with Henry.

The disaffection in south Germany and Saxony reached such dangerous proportions that the rebels summoned a council to judge Henry. At Tribur in October 1076 the humiliated Henry faced his accusers which included some of the very bishops who excommunicated Gregory eight months before. At this meeting the council informed Henry he would forfeit his kingdom if Gregory did not release him from excommunication within four months. Henry agreed to attend a council at Augsburg on 2 February 1077 where his fitness to rule would be debated. In order to put a legal cover over this treason against their king, the princes invited Gregory himself to "advise" them.

Henry never understood that the pope was part of a European-wide reforming trend. He simplistically believed that the rebellion of the nobles could be easily suppressed, Gregory could be driven out by imperial troops, and the dignity of his father's reign could be restored. First he must for diplomatic reasons be formally brought back into the church by the bishop of Rome who was on his way to the Augsburg council. In the past the issue would have been settled by seizing the person of the pope and installing an imperialist antipope. Circumstance compelled Henry to match wits not swords with Gregory. After escaping from Germany with his family Henry encountered the papal entourage in the mountains of Tuscany. At the castle of Canossa, where the pope was holed up fearing an imperial attack, Henry played the penitent sinner and stood barefoot in the snow begging absolution. Should the pope try to go to Augsburg to depose this incorrigible emperor or should he as a priest forgive this miserable Christian? The countess of Tuscany and the abbot of Cluny per-

suaded Gregory that the latter course was best for the
public image of the papacy. Although Henry, they
argued, would surely break his vow once back in Germany, the pope's magnanimous gesture as contrasted
with the emperor's treasonous ingratitude would prove
to the world who best deserved the honor of supreme
spiritual authority. This kind of moralistic reasoning
finally softened Gregory who after three days announced to the frostbitten penitent outside that he was
forgiven and received back into holy mother church.
Henry promised to abide by whatever would be decided
at Augsburg.

Henry's gamble at Canossa paid off. By removing the
stigma of excommunication he removed the princes'
legal pretext for rebellion. He could now attempt to
break up their coalition and crush them one at a time.
But from another perspective the emperor lost. For
while numerous popes had prostrated themselves, literally and figuratively, before emperors, never did an emperor so humble himself before a pontiff. The mystique
of theocratic kingship was buried in the snow at Canossa. Europe's collective memory was instilled with the
image of the majestic Holy Roman Emperor pleading
for forgiveness from the stern-faced pope. The deli-
cately balanced lever between the two universal rulers in
Christendom began to tilt towards Rome.

Despite this setback for the rebels a few princes were
determined to raise up their own king. Gregory, they
believed, double-crossed them by not going to Augsburg. When he heard of the anarchy north of the Alps
Gregory decided to turn back to Rome. At that, the
princes declared Henry deposed and elected one Rudolf
as the new king. During the bloody civil wars which
followed (1077-80), Rudolf and Henry both sought
Gregory's recognition. While the war in Germany saddened Gregory, he felt he could not immediately repudiate Rudolf's election lest he lose his leverage over
Henry. To recognize Rudolf would be to baptize an-

archy and rebellion. The church in Germany could never be reformed under such unstable conditions. Besides, Gregory did not believe that he had any basic right to direct secular rulers in their legitimate temporal concerns. Gregory did not consider his original deposition of Henry a final and definitive legal act, but rather a device to coerce Henry into assuming his proper role of defending the church and the empire.

In 1080 Gregory decided that Henry was hopelessly wicked and again pronounced him deposed; he recognized Rudolf conditionally as king. For his part, Henry called together his bishops of Germany and Lombardy and declared Gregory deposed for causing disorder in Italy and the empire. Henry had Clement III elected pope. There were now two emperors and two popes.

The papal star began to fade. Rudolf was killed in battle shortly after his diplomatic triumph over the pope. Spurred on by his recent victory over the allied princes in Saxony Henry led a large army over the Alps and laid siege to Rome. Gregory's popularity had by this time sunk so low that the Roman people blamed the pope for their difficulties. After repeated attempts the imperial army burst into the City and had Clement officially declared pope. The new pope then crowned Henry "Emperor Augustus of the Romans." In desperation Gregory asked the Normans to come to his rescue. But when the Norman soldiers arrived in Rome they proceeded to sack the City, despite Gregory's protests. For his own safety Gregory accompanied his "protectors" back to Sicily where he died in 1085, some said of a broken heart.

SETTLEMENT

Gregory's aggressive reform program brought him few friends and many enemies in Italy and Europe. Convinced that his dream had failed, Gregory's dying words were: "All my life I have fought iniquity, therefore I die in exile." In the short run Henry had vanquished his papal foe. The emperor had reestablished his temporal and ecclesiastical authority in Italy and Germany. But the victory proved illusive since Italian princes and prelates had learned to conspire with popes and friendly Germans. Back in Germany the barons discovered that alliances with popes could be useful in securing their own rights. The remainder of Henry's reign consisted of a confusing medley of alliances and counteralliances in Germany and Italy. The empire seemed impossible to hold together. Shortly before his death in 1106 Henry, still excommunicated, saw his own son and heir apparent raise the flag of revolt against him. The civil wars within Germany profited neither the emperor nor the pope. But the great princes emerged with more control over their principalities. The centralizing tendency of the German monarchy was halted by the investiture contest. Germany would have to wait until 1871 for political unification.

The specific issue of lay investiture was settled by a compromise in 1122. Emperor Henry V surrendered to the hierarchical church the right to invest prelates with the symbols of ring and staff. But the emperor could be present at the elections of bishops and abbots. Both sides saved face. The papacy won in principle, the emperor in practice. Needless to say the pope could never force the emperor or his representative to be absent from an ecclesiastical election in Germany. So the pope "granted"—a valuable precedent for later popes seeking restrictions on imperial authority—the emperor the right to be present at an election, a presence which virtually precluded a fair and canonical election. The compromise left many theoretical and practical problems unresolved but it did serve to temper imperial-papal quarrels for a time.

Conflicts over investitures continued after 1122 but the issue was rarely again confronted on the level of high principle. Church-state tensions assumed other forms.

PROPAGANDA WAR

The investiture controversy is significant not only for its effect on the Holy Roman Empire and on the papacy, but also for its influence on ideas. The period 1050-1122 was the first pamphlet war in European history. The supporters of Gregory and Henry turned out reams of literature in defense of their respective patrons. These pamphleteers realized that more than lay investiture was at stake. They asked: How should society be governed? Who was supreme ruler, emperor or pope? What are the jurisdictional limits of the church and the state? The answers to these questions left no person or institution untouched.

In this polemic literature two topics are prominent: (1) the origin of political power, and (2) the purpose of government.

Henry IV and his defenders agreed that the *origin* of legitimate political power was God. Beyond this common starting point, however, the imperialists were divided. How did God bestow His authority on the emperor? At least three replies were forthcoming: election, hereditary right, sanctified imperial office. To say that God delegated power to the king through the election of the great vassals had the advantage of putting the emperor beyond the reach of the papal arm. For if the princes chose their monarch, only they had the right to depose him. But this reasoning had the disadvantage of making the emperor accountable to the princes. The elector-princes would have a convenient pretext for rebellion against their emperor.

The argument from hereditary right was never a popular one among German princes, even though emperors in practice tried to establish dynasties. Ancient Germanic custom considered the king a first among equals, a functionary who could best protect the interests of the important men of the tribes.

The argument from divine officeship was Henry's most potent weapon. He was fond of displaying the ecclesiastical and religious aspects of his political office. He even dressed like a bishop during the grand ceremonies which accompanied important political events. The emperor was "king and priest," "king by the grace of God," "minister of God." God gave supreme power to David and Solomon, so he gave similar power to the present king. One of Henry's supporters was somewhat overenthusiastic when in a treatise he referred to the king as the vicar of Christ and as such he was superior to all churchmen even in spiritual matters. Since the king's office was theocratic and a part of the church hierarchy, why could he not invest bishops with their prelatal authority?

Gregory VII's reply was simple and direct. In his letters he insists that Christ entrusted His church to St Peter and his successors, the pontiffs. They must guide the church so that its members may attain heaven. All secular rulers within the church receive their authority from God through the church. Notice, say the papalists, who anoints the king: a bishop. Granted the king is somehow more than a layman, he is still not an ordained priest who preaches the gospel, says mass, and dispenses the sacraments. Since the church bestows the royal office on a particular layman, the church can take it away. (To this argument Henry could only reply that *custom* has made the office of the Holy Roman Emperor divine and sacrosanct. Clearly Henry was on the defense.)

Second, in addition to the origin of authority, the *purpose* of secular government was much discussed.

Henry's side attempted two different approaches while the papalists held mainly to a single solution.

On the one hand the more extreme imperialist writers dwell on the theocratic nature of Henry's status. Since the emperor is God's minister it follows that his main function is to safeguard His church. When Henry metes out justice in the realm he acts out of a desire to protect Christians and spread the true religion. His burning zeal for the gospel compels the emperor to ensure that the prelates (by lay investiture) are of the highest spiritual caliber.

On the other hand the moderate royalists try to cut the gordian knot by resorting to *dualism.* In society there are two spheres of authority, the spiritual and the temporal; each descends *directly* from God. The pope and the clergy tend to the former, the emperor the latter. Let the pope serve as a moral guide by his example and his prayers, while Henry minds the mundane affairs of everyday life. The pope has no business meddling in politics, just as the emperor should have no truck in priestly functions. Since many bishops and abbots acquire large landholdings with their offices, it is reasonable and just that the emperor have a say in the elections. After all he is the temporal lord of the empire, and ultimately the entire world. He needs loyal and competent men in high political positions. If the pope were a truly holy person he would leave the messy questions involving temporals to the emperor, lest the pontiff dilute his purity with worldliness.

Gregory's ideological offensive against these imperialist claims is devastating. To the theocratic defense of monarchy Gregory and his supporters answer that the emperor is still a layman beneath his cloak of majesty. As a layman he is subject to the clergy in spiritual matters. Of course the emperor's task is to punish sin and heresy, and to reform the church; this is the work assigned to the imperial office by the priests. The church anoints or creates an emperor to assist it in

Christianizing society. The church nods, the emperor executes the order. The "state," therefore, is not autonomous, but exists solely to help the pope and the clergy perform their spiritual work and prepare Christians for heaven. All the popes since St Peter, the first pope, have been the spiritual heads of Christendom. Christian kingship was a later, and man-made, invention. Moreover, who is to decide when a secular ruler is properly performing his function in coercing subjects? Clearly this decision should be made by the clergy, par excellence the pope, who gave the ruler such authority in the first place. The pope has the God-given responsibility to make sure that bishoprics are filled with God-fearing candidates whose thoughts are beyond this world.

To the dualist position of the royalists Gregory retorts that he did not have any intention of interfering in the normal running of temporal affairs. The papalists agree that the emperor's concern is indeed temporal and that the pope's concern is indeed spiritual. But the election of a bishop is not solely a temporal matter. As spiritual father, the pope has the right to make certain of the legality of episcopal elections, and of the worthiness of the episcopal candidate. If Henry accuses the pope of dabbling in "temporals," the latter will inform his imperial majesty where the line is drawn between the temporal and the spiritual in some doubtful case. Everyone admits that the line is frequently blurred. The function of government is to care for the bodies (material needs) of Christians; the pope looks after their souls (spiritual welfare). Just as the material is inferior to the spiritual, the worldly government is subservient to the papacy. Besides, who is to say that the pope cannot—when the church or the faith is in danger—occasionally settle a temporal case in the best interests of all?

AFTERMATH OF THE CONTROVERSY

Pamphlets have never determined the outcome of a power struggle. The investiture controversy would be settled on the battlefield and in the courts, not in the library. The revolutionary papalists were compelled by public opinion—and the need to placate their own consciences—to justify the Gregorian movement. While it is doubtful that the flood of imperialist as well as papalist propaganda ever converted anyone to either side, the written rationalizations proved useful to subsequent generations. The radical slogans shouted during the dispute would become the accepted axioms of the following century. What sounded so innovative in 1080 would be conventional by 1200.

The investiture struggle not only left a legacy of concepts, it forced educated and not so educated people to clarify their ideas of church and state. More and more one heard such questions as: just how much authority does a pope have? Time-worn clichés such as "king and priest" came under scrutiny. If the king calls himself a "priest" how does he differ from the local parish curé? This growing demand for sharp definition would soon ingrain in Europeans the habit of questioning and systematizing. It may be an exaggeration to say that the modern academic discipline called political science began in the Gregorian era, for politics was not yet pulled from its roots in theology and ecclesiology. But the breakthrough had been made. The energetic and sometimes visionary pamphleteers offered Europe a vocabulary and a methodology for dealing with church-state issues as ends in themselves. Finally, the feudal particularism of the early middle ages was irretrievably disturbed. Once thinkers fashioned their societal concerns in such cosmic abstractions as "temporal power" and "spiritual power" it would be impossible to pretend that the parochial problems of one's backyard could be solved, or even comprehended, in isolation from the larger social order. Before a Christendom could be built the concept had to be imagined.

It must be emphasized that the so-called investiture controversy was just one side of a religious revival. The

struggle makes no sense at all if it is seen as a mere
power contest between Henry and Gregory. The Gregorians, radical though they were, drew deeply from the
popular Cluniac reform tradition. The papal thrusts
stunned and confused consciences because many felt the
need for a visible pinnacle of authority. Many Germans
came to believe that the papacy, which posed less of an
immediate threat to private interests, was best suited to
direct the myriad of reforms in the interest of all. But
the century following 1000 witnessed movements other
than religious and ecclesiastical. After the anarchy of
the previous century the eleventh century occasioned a
population explosion, broadened cultural awareness,
increased food production, recovery of international
trade, and the expansion of cities. In any era rapid
change (in ideas, institutions, values) and fluidity pro-
duce a search for stability and reform ("Let's return to
the good old days"). Had Gregory VII appeared in the
tenth century he would have been dismissed as a harm-
less visionary. In the eleventh, Gregory's confident manner made fearful Christians willing to listen. It is no
coincidence that Gregory couched his legal and historical arguments for papal supremacy in moralistic terms.
Many demanded strong moral leadership which could
keep above politics. The world is sick, cried Hildebrand,
and is desperately in need of an immediate cure. Only
the rock of Peter can restore the peace of Christ.

CONCLUSION

From this analysis of the investiture contest between
the pope and the Holy Roman Emperor four conclusions can be drawn.

First, the clergy was conceptually freed from lay control. The clergy now formed a distinct body apart from
the laity. The "church" was no longer only the mass of
Christians; it was also the clerical "hierarchy" with its
own attitudes and laws. Once united and aware of its

distinct caste the clerical church proceeded to lead the rest of society.

Second, following the death of Gregory VII this church of priests was moving towards a centralized corporation headed by the *papacy*. Not only would the pope provide universal moral guidance, but the church was to be an *organization* realized in a tangible administration.

Third, the extreme papalists believed that they had restored the "right order." This divinely inspired order was a gradated society of authority: laymen, lower priests, bishops, pope. Charlemagne's scholars may have given life to the *idea* of Europe, but it was Gregory VII who attempted to institutionalize a political unit of Christians. With this noble attempt came "Christendom," Jesus' kingdom cast into an earthly form. This apocalyptic monarchy was conceived to be the human version of the structure of heaven.

Fourth, the (clerical) church began a movement to conquer the "state." For once the new activist clergy freed themselves from lay hegemony, they realized that they would have to consolidate their liberation by imposing controls. The clergy had to institutionalize the papal revolution. They tried to make the autonomous "state" into a department or function of the church. Thus the "state" had no public power of its own but had to restrict itself to the service of the spiritual power. What started as a withdrawal tactic to protect the clergy's spiritual interests slowly turned into a condition of superiority. It was hoped that lay rulers (the guardians of temporal needs) and priests (spiritual needs) would cooperate in their common attempt to save souls.

Gregory VII left behind an ideal only faintly realized while he lived. Conditions were not ready. But in the twelfth century his ideal of a papal Christendom found a Europe well-disposed to accept it.

We have in France one Peter Abelard, a monk without a rule, a persecutor of the Catholic church, an enemy of the cross of Christ.

Bernard of Clairvaux

II ————————————————————

PROPHETIC ALTERNATIVE: ABELARD AND BERNARD

PAPACY AFTER GREGORY VII

The Investiture Contest did not end with the death of Gregory VII in 1085. Kings and popes continued to collide over the elections of bishops and abbots. Once the widespread reaction to Gregory VII's extremism died down, the pontiffs found that their authority was mounting almost in spite of themselves. Three reasons account for this unexpected development.

First, the civil wars in Germany discredited the emperor's public image as the pacific universal ruler. While Henry IV whittled away his authority by his less-than-spiritual power struggles with popes, the German princes regained some of their ancient privileges.

Second, the unforeseen First Crusade (1096-99) did wonders for the prestige of the papal name. The spectacular success of this venture proved to all Christians that God had indeed willed the reconquest of Jerusalem and Bethlehem, the holiest places in Christendom. Surely God had appointed Pope Urban II (1088-99) to summon and organize such a glorious event.

Third, the papacy was creating the institutional means to implement the grandiose program of Hildebrand. Pope Urban II, a French noble who formerly resided at Cluny, reorganized the papal government along the centralized lines of Cluny and the royal court (curia) in France. He saw the papal office as a *monarchy* with the power to settle disputes among its "subjects." Accordingly Urban expanded the writing-office, financial administration, and the nonspiritual duties of the cardinals who were to head the rudimentary judicial and financial "departments." This low-keyed one-thing-at-a-time approach served to recover the papacy's credibility which had been damaged by Gregory VII's millenarian fantasies.

If a bishop, for example, felt his lands were being overtaxed (contrary to local custom) by the local prince or king, he had nothing to lose by appealing to the papal court in Rome. In the event the Roman court decided to hear the bishop's complaint the prince could retort that such a procedure was illegal and unprecedented. But as the pope's fame rose it became difficult for a prince, or anyone else, to deny God's liegeman the right to hear at least some cases. (Legal precedent was rarely a problem since the papal archivists could always find one.) The dam was broken. For once the *principle* of the papal right to litigate cases was universally recognized, it was an easy matter to enlarge the number of particular cases which could be heard.

By means of this slowly expanding administration the papacy was becoming a respected power. The popes' claim to be the successors of St Peter and rightful heads of the church gained acceptance as they handed down judicial opinions hammered out in the papal Curia. The more weighty issues were discussed in synods, which became models for effective administration. The pope announced his legal opinions in the form of decretals which were incorporated into canon or church law. Having his own staff of personal legates and a body of law, the Holy Father entered the world political arena as a formidable power. Gregory VII would probably have approved of this development by arguing from the need to maintain the freedom of the church from lay interference.

It must not be thought that twelfth-century popes unilaterally seized control of the church. The opposite is true, for this control was largely *given* to them. Since Europe was a complex network of conflicting legal jurisdictions, men gradually saw the social *usefulness* of a final court of appeal. No lords, prelates, or townsmen had any intention of relinquishing authority when they filed law suits in Rome. Rather, they sought to exploit the papacy's growing reputation for efficient and impartial justice—whenever they believed Rome would rule in their favor. This popular demand for more rulings from Rome indirectly spun the papacy's vast bureaucratic web throughout Europe. But few (at least in the early twelfth century) complained of the pope's increasing power, since the Curia as a final court of appeal served a vital function in providing a semblance of order and rationality in an anarchic feudal and urban society.

Gone were the days when popes were expected to parade their contempt for this world. After Gregory VII the papacy was committed to the activist role of guiding, organizing, and Christianizing the whole of society.

FRANCE

France after 1100 was restless. The French nobility was still gloating in its recent military success in the Holy Land in 1099. But the incessant reprimands from the higher clergy were giving fighting a bad name. More telling on the petty nobility were the encroachments of the great princes, secular and ecclesiastical, who were making civil wars among lesser nobles more risky. Moreover, the French nobility found itself caught in the middle of economic transition. The population upsurge, increased food production, growth of towns, and accelerated flow of goods and currency caused a strain on those social institutions which were born in a time of simpler agrarian conditions. The nobles could sometimes band together in spirit, and could even invent a "class" literature (feudal epics and courtly love romance) to ward off real or imagined threats to their privileged status; but they could not wield themselves into a unit for effective political and moral leadership. Long centuries of feudal anarchy had left their mark. The rural noble was too addicted to his personal sense of honor, love of fighting (when not engaged in battle he fought in neighborhood tournaments), and loyalty to his local lord and/or his family to be good for much else. With apprehension he observed the rising power of the great princes, the hierarchical church, and the urban classes.

The dynamism of the rapidly changing society of the early twelfth century was fed especially by two interrelated movements: *educational* and *religious*. The urban cathedral schools, forerunners of the thirteenth-century universities, tried to furnish the new learning demanded by vagabond scholars and by bishops and princes who both required trained administrators. As best they could, the towns and courts tried to accommodate this influx of students. The result was not an educational system, but a patchwork of informal floating classrooms which revolved less around institutions than about individual professors.

The religious movements were just as fervent and just as amorphous. The socioeconomic tensions in the towns and countryside rendered unstable persons susceptible to firebrand preachers with strange doctrines. In the towns and courts interest in theological and philosophical questions ran high. While this interest sometimes stemmed from a shallow dilettantism it oftentimes coincided with intense religious devotion and desire for church reform. The church had no chance to control these chaotic religious forces, for in a sense the church *was* these forces. The church formed no monolithic structure; the powers ascribed to bishops and priests varied widely. There were conflicting opinions, even among bishops, on every aspect of the Catholic faith. But more Christians were coming to believe in the desirability of a visible clerical hierarchy which taught a clear-cut single doctrine.

But the aristocrats would not answer the call to educational and religious leadership. Their own self-image and the peculiar socioeconomic institutions of the time disqualified them from the role of disinterested stewardship. The question of early twelfth-century France remained: who would step in to take a firm hold on the myriad of institutional, social, and intellectual directions? Would the bishops, the obvious candidates for the task, furnish such guidance? Too many of them, alas, were overly concerned with petty politics and local affairs. Their parish priests were too ignorant and parochial-minded to be of much assistance in any massive episcopal effort. Would the Lord's anointed, the king of the Franks, offer a rallying point? He was as yet too weak. Then what about the professors in the new schools and the monks of the countryside? These two groups, the natural top layers of the fast-moving educa-

tional and religious movements were surprised although
not displeased to see how quickly their advice was
sought.

CONFLICT BETWEEN ABELARD AND BERNARD

The twelfth century witnessed the fertile interplay
between two bands of teachers, the intellectuals of the
cathedral schools and the new ascetic monks. Abelard
best exemplifies the former group, Bernard of Clairvaux
the latter. Abelard wanted the professors to assume
leadership in the church; Bernard the monks. But the
world proved too small for these two self-proclaimed
prophets. They clashed at the Council of Sens in 1140.
From the broader perspective of Europe's church-state
relations, however, Abelard and Bernard had something
in common: they both represented alternatives to the
Gregorian steamroller. In the end, the twin movements
in religion and education were absorbed into the papalized church.

PETER ABELARD (1079-1142)

Peter Abelard was born in a small town in Brittany in
1079. His father, Berengar, a knight in the service of the
count of Brittany, tutored his young son in the liberal
arts. Since Peter was the eldest son and heir to the family estates, it came as a surprise and a disappointment to
Berengar to learn that Peter did not intend to become a
knight and a landlord. Instead he wanted to continue his
education at one of the nearby schools and perhaps enter the priesthood. Respectful of his son's wishes Berengar sent Peter off on his uncertain career. It is a commentary on the openness of twelfth-century French
society that Abelard, one of the outstanding geniuses of
the middle ages, came from an obscure castle in Brittany.

After attending several schools in northwestern France Abelard became bored. He discovered how easily he could surpass his fellow students in the subjects of classical literature and dialectic. The mathematical sciences he found uninteresting. Being self-conscious of his humble background Abelard felt a neurotic compulsion to exhibit his cleverness at the expense of his class-mates—and his professors. While his feeling of insecurity drove him to study harder than the other students he acquired a reputation for being an eccentric loner. Much to the relief of his exasperated instructors Abelard set out to study dialectic in Paris where the cathedral school was reputed to be the finest in the land.

This uncouth but precocious youth soon fell out with his Parisian teachers. Not content with small-fry, Abelard challenged William of Champeaux, archdeacon of the cathedral school of Notre Dame and the foremost master in the city. In Abelard's own words: "I forced him [William] by clear proofs from reasoning to change, yes, to abandon his old stand on universals." William was a "realist" in the problem of "universals." He held that a "universal," e.g., the concept of "man," existed in itself apart from individuals, e.g., particular men such as Hildebrand. Typically, Abelard went to the opposite extreme by advocating a nominalism which made the individual the ultimate reality. (Later Abelard found a mean between these two extreme positions.) After having been made the fool, "William's lectures bogged down into such carelessness that they could scarcely be called lectures on logic at all." Soon William's class-rooms were nearly empty as students flocked to listen to the young student who dared to attack the venerable old master. Since licenses to teach (when they were needed at all) were informally distributed, it was possible for an articulate student to hold his own classes, provided he could get pupils to pay him. As the number of Abelard's disciples multiplied, the humiliated William resigned. But a few days later, William (out of revenge, according to Abelard) had Abelard dismissed on trumped up charges.

Abelard set up a rival "free university" at Melun, but soon returned to Paris. After more encounters with William, Abelard emerged as the undisputed master of philosophy at Paris. Abelard's superciliousness may have alienated him from the cathedral administration and faculty, but his popularity among the students made him untouchable. Besides, a magnetic teacher could bolster the reputation (and the enrollments) of the cathedral school.

Possibly at the urging of his mother, Abelard left teaching and decided to study theology. Since Anselm of Laon was the most famous theologian in the kingdom, Abelard enrolled as a divinity student at Laon to sit at the feet of the master. But Abelard soon found that the old man "had a remarkable command of language, but it was despicable with respect to meaning and devoid of sense." Leaving Anselm's class in disgust, Abelard, who had no training in the sacred science, began to hold his own lectures on Scripture. These lectures became so popular that the indignant Anselm had Abelard expelled. Anselm's rough handling of Abelard made this maverick something of a folk hero to the students; they came to prefer Abelard's fresh approach to that of the safe but dull lectures of the white-haired father.

Back in Paris Abelard wasted no time in establishing himself as the leading theologian at the school. Of himself Abelard said, "I considered myself . . . the one philosopher in the world." At this time Abelard met Heloise.

HELOISE

A canon of Notre Dame named Fulbert persuaded Abelard, now about 40, to tutor his niece Heloise, about 17. Herself a prodigy, Heloise was well known around

Paris for her learning. Abelard did not mind taking the
extra time to instruct her since it meant some extra cash
and the potentially useful friendship of a canon. So
impressed at her progress in letters and her pleasant conversation, he decided (possibly at Heloise's suggestion)
to ask Fulbert to permit him to lodge in a quiet study in
his house. Proud and flattered to have the renowned
Abelard as a house guest, Fulbert readily agreed and
even encouraged him to punish her if she proved sloth-
ful.

Abelard's admiration for Heloise as a student soon
became an admiration for her as a woman. Gradually
they drifted from intellectual companionship to another
level of love.

> We were first together in one house and then in one mind.
> Under the pretext of work we made ourselves entirely free
> for love. . . . We opened our books but more words of love
> than of the lesson asserted themselves. There was more kiss-
> ing than teaching: my hands found themselves at her
> breasts more often than on the book. . . . No sign of love
> was omitted by us in our ardor.

Abelard gave less and less time to his lectures.

> It became wearisome for me to go there [school] and
> equally hard to stay when I was using nightly vigils for love
> and the days for study. I became negligent and indifferent
> in my lectures so that nothing I said stemmed from my
> talent but I repeated everything from rote.

Abelard the philosopher became Abelard the poet. He
wrote no longer of philosophy but of his beloved. (A
few years later these verses would be sung in the courts
and in the streets throughout the realm.) At first Fulbert tried to ignore the town gossip, but he finally pressured the lovers to reveal their secret. Disappointed in
Abelard and in his niece, the infuriated Fulbert drove
Abelard from his home. When Heloise wrote to Abelard
informing him of her pregnancy he had her secretly hurried off to his sister's home in Brittany where a boy,
Astrolabe, was born. To appease Fulbert, Abelard prom-

ised to marry Heloise, provided that the marriage be performed in secret to protect Abelard's reputation as a teacher-scholar. Since Abelard was only a tonsured cleric he could legally marry, but custom demanded that a teacher of philosophy and theology be an unmarried priest. Clerical celibacy was by no means universal at the time, but it was usually expected of a cathedral school professor who trained priests and future priests.

Against the wishes of Heloise, who did not want to destroy Abelard's career, they married in the presence of Fulbert. To save face, Fulbert began to make the marriage public, contrary to his promise. Heloise suffered much abuse by her refusal to acknowledge publicly that she was married. She and Abelard agreed that the best solution for the moment was for her to enter a convent outside Paris. Heloise had no inclination to enter the religious life but she was persuaded that any other course would be injurious to her husband.

When Fulbert learned of this latest development he accused Abelard of trying to get rid of Heloise and put him to shame. In retaliation, a band of Fulbert's relatives fell upon Abelard in his bed one night and "they cut off the organs by which I had committed the deed which they deplored." Broken in body and soul Abelard became a monk at the Benedictine abbey of St Denis just north of Paris. Abelard's pride never recovered from these traumatic events. He now needed a respite from human affairs.

THE WANDERING MONK

But no sooner had Abelard settled down in his new home than he found himself publicly chastising the worldly lives of the monks at St Denis. Anxious to silence this foreigner in their midst the monks permitted Abelard to retire to a priory to set up a school. His confidence restored, Abelard resumed teaching and writing on theological issues. Once again his success brought him ardent admirers. Abelard's well-known love affair did not lessen the esteem of their hero. On the contrary, the scandal made the towering Abelard appear all the more exciting and enigmatic.

Abelard wrote a book, *On the Unity and Trinity of God**, in answer to requests from his students who demanded rational explanations of the Christian faith. Abelard and a small group of theologians at the time believed that a Christian could live his faith more fully if he understood the tenets of his religion. To act solely on blind faith could be detrimental to faith. To be sure Abelard did not hold that the dogma of the Trinity, or any other dogma, had to be grasped by reason *before* it could be accepted by faith. Indeed, he condemned some of his academic collegues for just this brand of extreme rationalism. Abelard's more modest task was to demonstrate the inherent plausibility of Christian Revelation. While a mere human could never fully penetrate the divine mysteries, he could convince himself that nothing in Christianity is contrary to reason. To believe in the notion of the Trinity is so natural and so reasonable that Plato himself, Abelard assures us, came close to comprehending it—as far as this was possible for a pagan.

In his treatise Abelard sought to legitimize dialectic. By using dialectic a Christian could fortify his faith and be capable of convincing others of its validity. To make the Trinity seem plausible, Abelard presented his readers with similes taken from daily experience. Abelard was not an armchair theologian locked away in an ivory tower. He was mainly concerned with the lives of real people, particularly his students. He sought to make their religion—frequently learned at home by rote—relevant to their existing problems. Abelard observed students wavering in a faith which seemed empty and out of touch with the urban scene. Their religion was

*Modern scholars usually refer to this work as the *Theologia 'Summi Boni'*.

molded during an earlier era when external observances
were stressed. Abelard feared that the current rage for
dialectic might tempt students to forget Jesus and His
message. He wanted to show them that Catholicism was
not a maze of superstitious practices, but a living faith
which made dialectic all the more intriguing, and vice
versa. Faith and reason are one. This ability to fuse
dialectic and theology accounts for Abelard's enormous
popularity as a teacher and scholar.

Traditionalist theologians were scandalized, or pre-
tended to be, by Abelard's *On the Unity and Trinity.*
They said it contained numerous heresies including the
blasphemy that there are three Gods. Moreover, Abelard
presumed to interpret church doctrine without relying
sufficiently on the standard authorities such as St
Augustine. In the early twelfth century it was difficult
to convict a professor on the charge of heresy because
of the shapeless state of Christian doctrine. An active
sower of social dissention, however, could be easily
branded a heretic and hunted down, since no self-
respecting noble or rich townsman would openly defend
a social revolutionary. A theologian could almost never
be "officially" censured—unless he had enough enemies
determined to ensnare him. Abelard had more than
enough adversaries who finally were able to rig a condemnation of his teachings at the Council of Soissons in
1121. At this council Abelard was forced to burn his
book with his own hand.

Having agreed at the council never to join another
monastery Abelard turned his back on the world and
became a hermit in Champagne. There he built a chapel
which he named the Paraclete (or the Comforter, a
name St John gives to the Holy Spirit). But solitude
was not to be his vocation, for as Abelard's whereabouts
became known, students rushed to his hiding place in
the woods. As usual, Abelard's contact with students
inspired him and stimulated him to write. His enemies

despaired: is there no way to stop the spread of the Abelard infection?

In 1126 Abelard's relative tranquillity was interrupted. Knowing of his fame, some monks in Brittany asked him to become their abbot. Could this request be a summons from God—and the attainment of peace of mind? Like a fugitive, Abelard fled to this obscure monastery to begin a new life. Self-righteous and tactless as ever, he soon infuriated the lax monks by attempting to restore discipline in the monastery. Exasperated with Abelard's zeal, a few of the brethren poisoned the wine he was to drink at mass. After several years of this dangerous game he finally stomped out of the monastery in disgust.

Meanwhile the Abbot Suger of St Denis had Heloise and her nuns driven out of Argenteuil—the pretext being the alleged immorality of the nuns cloistered there. With the permission of Pope Innocent II, the count of Champagne, and the local bishop, Abelard donated the Paraclete to the displaced sisters. When Abelard's autobiography, appropriately titled *Story of my Misfortunes*, fell beneath Heloise's eyes she wrote Abelard asking about his recent activities. The letters exchanged between them reveal their extraordinary capacity for selfless love and introspection.

ABELARD'S NEW CHURCH

Throughout these wanderings Abelard's writings were widely read—to the delight of some, the horror of others. One of his earlier works, *Yes and No*, marked Abelard as one of the daring young dialecticians who inhabited the cathedral schools of the cities. Following a recently established tradition, Abelard listed, without commentary, propositions from venerable church authorities in two columns, for and against. In one column Abelard selected passages which seem to support the statement: "Christ alone is the foundation of the church," or "without baptism of water no one can be saved," or "it is permitted to kill men." In the other he enumerated quotes defending the opposite view: "Christ alone is not the foundation of the church," etc. Typically, Abelard sometimes chose topics as much for their shock effect as for their intrinsic theological interest. By these tactics Abelard had no intention of demonstrating contradictions inherent in the church authorities and the Scriptures. On the contrary, he intended to show, as he pointed out in the prologue to *Yes and No*, that no contradictions exist once the wording of the quotations is carefully studied. One must not complacently accept these bald assertions on blind faith. One must analyze the *historical context* in which these formulations were made in order to grasp the intention of the writers, and to illustrate the essential unity of the true faith. Abelard agreed that while truth is indeed changeless, it must be *restated* to fit the times, so that Christians can comprehend the truth which lies behind the human formulation (language, a man-made artifact) of its meaning.

What perturbed many readers of the *Yes and No* was that Abelard seemed to be mocking Christianity by implying that there were contradictions in the true religion. Besides, why inquire into the meaning of Christian Revelation, for was it not laid out in the Scriptures and the Fathers once for all? Dogma was not a subject to be dissected before the ignorant like arithmetic; it was to be accepted docilely. Faith is to be lived, not scrutinized. If this mere professor undermines the moral authority of the Fathers, how long will it be before he presumes to usurp the legitimate authority of bishops and popes—the hierarchy established by Christ—and destroy their status as leaders in the church? Abelard's free-swinging style appeared to these protectors of the faith (which included other professors and monks as well as the ordinary ecclesiastical hierarchy) to endanger the purity and orthodoxy of the absolute truth.

While these obscurantist critics might have exaggerated the dangers to the church arising from the new dialectic, they correctly perceived the root issue. In their artless way they accused Abelard of subverting the Catholic church. For them, the church was grounded either in monastic spirituality (with its emphasis on detachment and a personalist, contemplative approach to Scripture) or in Gregorian papalism. The former stressed the moral leadership provided by the holy man of the cloisters, while the latter (as yet, not a potent force in northern France) centered on the papal-episcopal leadership with its links in canon law, organization, and secular politics.

While monks and bishops saw Christian society from varying sides, they agreed that Abelard by his actions and books was advocating a *new concept of the church.* Abelard in fact was quite willing to leave church structures untouched. What concerned him was the "outside" group which stimulated this structure to keep it God-oriented. The *professors of the urban schools* would replace the Benedictine monks (who would still exist in this utopian world) in the role of gadfly to the organizational church. The professors would stir up discussion regarding Revelation, and teach Christians how to apply Christian principles to their own lives. The professors would show that Christian doctrine is not a static set of precepts to be "protected," but a part of the creative process in human history. And who would be better qualified to give witness to this divine progress than the theology and philosophy professors who are not bogged down with vested economic and political interests in the established church? God gave special intellectual powers to a predestined few who would perform this important function in the church universal.

Abelard, then, envisioned a *new elite* which was to guide the *ecclesia.* To be sure this new brand of clerical evangelists would be subservient to the ordinary hierarchy of the church, with whom they would work in uni-

son. The bishops would tend to church discipline and
run the mundane affairs of the church. They would punish heresy and act as spiritual directors to all Christians.
The new prophets, on the other hand, would train the
intellectually gifted to inquire into the mysteries of the
truth. At the same time these trained specialists, who
almost always would be better Christians for their sharp-
ened intellects, would act as witnesses for Christ to laymen. This "second clergy" would provide charismatic
guidance to a church always in need of reformation.
Thus the cathedral school teacher was for Abelard not
merely a classroom instructor, but a church functionary
who determined Christian values for the total society.

Within this new church the state would have a special
place. In discussing the sacrament of unction Abelard
refers to the relation of the priest to the king: "in the
unction of the feet the lesser person is signified, i.e., the
priest; in that of the head, the greater, i.e., the king."
Abelard did not arrive at this exalted notion of kingship
through a detached analysis of political theory, a subject
which did not interest him. Rather, his generally amica-
ble encounters with Louis VI (1108-37) and Louis VII
(1137-80) convinced him of the value of royal protection vis-à-vis his clerical enemies. On several occasions
the French monarch sheltered Abelard from the wrath
of prelates and abbots (although Abelard did have
admirers in high church offices). From Louis VI's view,
a popular scholar in Paris was good for the prestige of
his court; such a teacher could prove politically useful in
playing one faction in the church against another.

Abelard's attitude towards the temporal power was
basically conservative. The king was essentially a feudal
suzerain whose task it was to protect local custom and
to govern his own domains. The king, guardian of the
status quo, should never attempt to ride roughshod over
the legitimate rule of dukes, counts, and prelates in the
realm. But Abelard also believed that the king had an
emergency function in church affairs: to safeguard the

liberty of theologians and philosophers. Ordinarily the king should keep his hands off clerical affairs and matters spiritual. But in those instances when bishops or monks attempted to hamper one of God's elect from speculating on divine knowledge, the king, as God's instrument, was obligated to leave the temporal sphere and shelter the persecuted teacher.

Around 1135 Abelard resumed teaching despite his condemnation at Soissons in 1121. In an age when monks felt their moral predominance threatened and, at the same time, when they tried to comprehend a rapidly changing world, they began to cast about for simplistic explanations. Surely the new learning in the city schools was largely to blame for these troubled times. If only someone could silence the incorrigible Abelard—as a warning to future would-be Abelards—the magisterial church could regain control over heretical movements and feudal violence.

BERNARD OF CLAIRVAUX (1090-1153)

In about 1138 the Benedictine monk William of St Thierry happened upon one of Abelard's theological works. A convert to the new Cistercian asceticism, William was thunderstruck by the "heresies" he discovered in the book. Immediately William drew up a list of the most offensive passages in Abelard's tract and asked his friend Bernard to appraise them. In his emotional appeal to his spiritual brother, William hinted that only he, Bernard, was capable of eradicating Abelard's "heresy" which was about to "destroy the church."

Bernard replied that he had not read Abelard's writings but he would look into the matter after Easter. When Bernard finally found the time to peruse Abelard's works he came to share William's concern and agreed, tentatively, to take up the challenge. Thus began the battle of the giants.

St Bernard of Clairvaux stamped his personality on
Europe. During the period 1130-52 the pivot of Europe
was Clairvaux, not Rome. While Abelard may have persuaded many, especially his young students, to accept
his interpretations of Scripture and to adopt his methodology, rarely could he command important people to
do his will. Indeed, Abelard seemed a passive plaything
in the hands of the powerful; his intellectual legacy
would not be fully apparent until after his death. After
Abelard was twice condemned by some clergymen, even
scholars were hesitant to admit the extent of his influence on their thought. But Bernard of Clairvaux appeared on top of events; he compelled men to immediate action. Bernard chose popes, summoned a crusade,
reprimanded kings. The abbot of Clairvaux alone decided which matter, ecclesiastical or secular, fell under
his purview. When this man of God approached, the
mighty of the world trembled.

Bernard was born in 1090 in a castle near Dijon. His
father, Tescelin, was a vassal and a friend of the duke of
Burgundy. His mother, Aleth, was a descendent of the
ducal line itself. As was typical of a family of high nobility, at least one son, in this case Bernard, was selected to
enter the church—for God and family fortune. Since a
would-be bishop or abbot or other high church official
needed training in theology and administrative skills,
Tescelin sent the boy Bernard to a nearby school run by
canons regular. Contemporary accounts describe Bernard as tall, blond, and handsome. Although well-
mannered and urbane, he was introspective and felt
uncomfortable in extended polite conversation. Bernard's mother, a devout even puritanical Christian,
imbued in her son strong religious sensibilities and a
feeling of unworthiness; Bernard would always experience pangs of guilt for not having given enough of himself to his Lord. Tescelin, about whom little is known,
may have been a more conventional kind of Christian
although more pious than most of his social class. He

passed on to his impressionable offspring that sense of
self-righteous duty—to God, other nobles, the poor—
which was appropriate for one of high birth.

As a youth Bernard heard marvelous stories of
knights in armor fighting for Christ in the Holy Land.
But Bernard's sensitive temperament and uncertain
health were unsuited for soldiering. He passionately
wanted to devote himself totally to Christ—but without
ceasing to be a knight. How can a knight serve Christ
without engaging in the secular activity of war? Shortly
after his mother's death Bernard solved his difficulty.
Like Abelard he would reject the path chosen for him
by his father. Never one for half measures, Bernard
turned away from a future of study or high office in the
church to a life of absolute self-denial. He had heard of
a few young nobles dwelling in the swamps outside
Dijon in a hermitage called Citeaux.

CITEAUX VS. CLUNY

Citeaux was founded in 1098 by Robert de Molesme
as a place for uninterrupted prayer. Robert sought to
live the Rule of St Benedict (d. 547) to the letter. Here
Robert and his tiny band put into practice the monastic
vows of poverty, chastity, and obedience. In the swamp
of Citeaux these monks lived a simple routine of prayer
(private and collective), hard manual work, and bodily
penances.

Citeaux, an offshoot of the evangelical revival of the
eleventh century, was partially a reaction to Cluny. (The
Cluniac movement prepared the way for Pope Gregory
VII's reforms.) Cluny began in 910 as an attempt to
liberate monasteries from the grasp of local lay lords; by
1100 Cluny was part of the cozy establishment church.
Cluniac monasteries had gradually acquired enormous
landed wealth and political influence. They represented
a culture rich in art, music, and letters. Cluniacs justified
their comfortable life-styles by insisting on the need to

"modernize" and "adapt" the Benedictine Rule to new situations.

When Bernard decided upon his unusual vocation he took with him to Citeaux thirty friends and relatives—including his uncle and five of his six brothers. Tescelin must have felt the blessing of God or the curse of Satan upon hearing the news of the peculiar exodus. Bernard not only discovered an answer to his search for personal fulfillment, he discovered that he was a leader. For the remainder of his life Bernard's extraordinary self-confidence enabled him to pursue his goals with un-flinching single-mindedness. Surely anyone, he believed, who could convince proud nobles to abandon the world and dedicate their lives to God must have had divine assistance.

The appearance of Bernard and his recruits gave en-couragement to the monks at Citeaux. Here Bernard worked in the fields, studied the Bible, chanted the office with his brothers. At this isolated spot in the woods these happy monks wished only to dedicate their lives to God, apart from worldly distractions. Realizing Bernard's talents the abbot of Citeaux sent him with twelve monks, including three of his brothers, to found another monastery in Burgundy. Bernard chose a deso-late site 70 miles from Citeaux and named it Clairvaux, or Valley of Light. For the rest of his life Clairvaux would remain his spiritual home, an oasis in a world of turmoil.

But this peace was disrupted when Bernard's younger cousin, Robert, left the relative comforts of Cluny to become a monk at nearby Clairvaux. Distressed at this loss, the prior of Cluny went to Clairvaux and persuaded the boy to return with him to Cluny. When Bernard learned what had happened he penned a volcanic letter ostensibly intended for Robert but actually directed at the whole Cluniac way of life. Bernard accused the prior of preaching a "new Gospel." The prior, continued Ber-nard, "commended feasting and condemned fasting. He called voluntary poverty wretched and poured scorn upon fasts, vigils, silence, and manual labor." Bernard blasted the Cluniacs for prostituting the original principles laid down by St Benedict. With this open attack on Cluny Bernard began the public phase of his career. Henceforth the abbot of Clairvaux emerged as the undisputed leader of the Cistercian (from the word Citeaux) movement. By constantly reprimanding the Cluniacs Bernard strenghtened the resolve of his Cistercian brethren who gradually became aware of their special mission in Christendom.

In the 1120s Bernard founded numerous daughter houses of Clairvaux to accommodate the rush to the new order. Bernard was successful in persuading droves of young nobles to enter Cistercian monasteries. Cluniacs and Cistercians vied with each other for recruits and legal privileges. Albeit with an uneasy conscience Bernard soon found himself battling princes, bishops, and Cluniacs in defense of besieged Cistercian communities. The many friendships he formed with prelates and abbots would prove useful in his later dispute with Abelard. Before 1130 Bernard could justify these distractions as necessary evils in the struggle for the survival of the newly implanted Cistercian centers.

Bernard wrestled with a dilemma. A Cistercian was by definition a contemplative who dwelt apart from worldly cares. But how should a Cistercian respond to the church? Since the Cistercian was a near-perfect Christian, was he not obliged to step forward and point out the solutions for sinful men who were too blind to perceive the church's ills and who were too weak to correct them? After all, the monk's task was not only to save his own soul, but also those who live in the world. But how can God's elect purify the world without becoming themselves corrupted by it?

This predicament was resolved for Bernard in 1130, the year he entered the European stage. Before this date Bernard's name was associated with the world of monas-

ticism. This time it was clearly not a question of safeguarding only the brethren, but all Christians.

SCHISM (1130-37)

When Pope Honorius died in 1130 the cardinals divided their loyalties between the two most powerful
Roman families, the Frangipani and the Pierleoni. After
some maneuvering by the papal chancellor a small group
of cardinals raised a member (who took the name of
Innocent II) of the Frangipani household to the apostolic see *before* Honorius died—contrary to canon law.
When the Pierleoni learned they had been outwitted
they quickly elected their own leader to the Chair of
Peter under the name of Anaclet. Innocent II soon realized how slim his support was in the City and so he fled
from Italy to find aid beyond the Alps. Innocent II
made a good beginning by getting the recognition of the
abbot of Cluny—and the abbot of Clairvaux.

Bernard showed no hesitation in deciding who was
true pope. A continued schism in the papacy, Bernard
believed, would prove disruptive to the church. Bernard
justified his exodus from the monastery by pointing out
that "God's business" allowed it. Bernard must convince
the princes of Christendom—who straddled the fence
with a view to maximum political advantage—that God's
choice lay in Innocent. For the next seven years the
fiery Bernard, who led Innocent from town to town
throughout Europe, harangued and cajoled kings,
barons, bishops, abbots, and townspeople to get them to
recognize the legitimacy of the Frangipani candidate. So
effective was Bernard that when Anaclet died in 1137
the king of Sicily was the only non-Roman prince who
remained faithful to the Pierleoni; the rest came out for
Innocent. The will of God had prevailed.

During the schism Bernard penned innumerable letters. In a letter to the bishops of Aquitaine Bernard
speaks of a crusade against the Forces of Darkness.

Those who choose Anaclet choose Antichrist and the Devil. This long letter is less a request to consider the legal merits of Innocent's election than it is an emotionally-charged sermon which commands the bishops to take up their immediate responsibilities. Writing in the tone of an angry father correcting his wayward children, Bernard berates their caution and threatens them with eternal damnation. Bernard warns that their failure to condemn the foes of Innocent will result in the triumph of the Prince of this world.

How can the bishops of Aquitaine be assured that Innocent is true pope? Bernard gives three criteria for determining the will of God. First, Innocent II was elected according to the church's law, while Anaclet was not. (Bernard simplifies the confused circumstances surrounding the separate elections of Innocent and Anaclet; both elections in fact were canonically irregular.)

Second, Bernard contends that all the important prelates and princes in Europe acknowledge Innocent as the "judgment of God." It would be political suicide, hints Bernard, not to get on such a formidable bandwagon. But aside from any political advantage to be won, Bernard emphasizes the *sanctity* of those who recognize Innocent. The holier the Christian, the more clearly he can perceive the Lord's wishes. But not only do virtuous prelates perceive God's choice, so do monks. Since these religious orders (especially the Cistercians) are "dead to this world" and have "eyes fully open to God's will," their consent proves beyond any doubt that Innocent is the one. Only monks—less from their official status than from their interior disposition—have that special mystical knowledge which is found in prayer.

Third, as a corollary to the above, Innocent is himself a good Christian. Therefore he must be true pope. As Bernard puts it: "which of these two men seems to be the pope?" It is evident to all that "the character and good name of Innocent need fear no comparison with that of his adversary." Bernard will not hear of another election, for it will certainly be rigged. If Innocent's own character is not enough, look at the virtuous lives of the Romans who elected him. Only "sinful" men chose Anaclet, a tool of Satan.

Was Bernard so naive as to think that disputed elections in the church could be settled by references to the candidates' personal characters? How could the contestants' "virtue" be determined? Bernard's peculiar view was in fact widespread among the ascetical-minded in monasteries and even among some prelates in Rome.

In partial opposition to the Gregorian emphasis on a legally constituted clerical church Bernard wanted Christian society to be directed by *prophets*. Ideally these messengers of God should fill the offices of the papacy and the episcopacy. Their chief function should be to provide edifying examples for other Christians. These charismatic leaders should direct men and women to heaven by their own virtuous lives, not by overinvolvement in church administration and finance. The extreme Gregorian view of the papacy placed the pope at the head of a giant bureaucracy which controlled many matters concerning dogma, discipline, ecclesiastical courts, crusades, benefices, privileges, education, relations with lay princes—and certain temporal affairs previously the domain of the princes.

Because popes and bishops were tainted with the material world, said Bernard, the church needs contemplative monks—par excellence, the Cistercians—who gave witness to absolute detachment and who kept this ideal of poverty before the eyes of churchmen. Monks must never volunteer to straighten out the organizational church. Rather, it is the popes or bishops who *summon* monks to lend assistance. Thus the church beckoned Bernard to employ his prophetic powers to reunite the troubled church. Since Bernard the prophet was God's voice crying out in the world—Bernard frequently referred to his own directives as "God's will"—, he was in

effect ordered by God to notify the bishops of Aquitaine which of the papal contenders was His choice.

Bernard's view of the church was attractive at the
time because it was linked to the past. Aristocrats felt at
home with a spirituality which derived from a feudal-
military ethic (the good knight engages evil in armed
combat), an ethic nostalgic of a half-legendary past
when the nobility ruled a merry Christendom. These
elect of God were attuned to the then current revival of
an otherworldly approach to religion—which was simul-
taneously a reproach to the worldly lives of many prelates. Bernard's stress on individual mystical experience
served as an antidote to the growing power of the great
princes. Bernard tried to synthesize the monastic tradition with the outlook of the feudal nobility.

Bernard was no revolutionary. The well-meaning
abbot wanted only to infuse life into existing ecclesiastical structures. He was willing to accept the basic frame
of the Gregorian church, but he also wanted to temper
the spreading legalism within the clerical body. Bernard's anachronistic conception of society, however,
ignored the hard facts of urbanization, scholastic education, and canon law. Bernard's narrow vision prevented
him from appreciating the valuable social services provided by the papal Curia.

In short, Bernard justified the monk's occasional
involvement in church politics on the basis of his interpretation of God's Kingdom. Most monks in the early
middle ages believed in the transitory nature of temporal things and the futility of human action. Since the
world will soon cease to exist, why bother to try to
improve it? Bernard disagreed. The monk must try to
preserve (ordinarily by his prayer and his personal example, extraordinarily by his intervention) the temporal
kingdom of God, for it is the archetype of the Kingdom
of God in heaven. As Christ is the King of the heavenly

realm, the pope, Christ's lieutenant, is the king of the
earthly realm.

BERNARD CHALLENGES ABELARD

Shortly after Bernard's success in installing Innocent
II in 1137, he received the letter from William of St
Thierry summoning him to yet another combat. Although Bernard was now a seasoned warrior and the
most powerful single person in Christendom, he hesitated before this fresh challenge. Yes, Bernard had taken
on heresy before, but Abelard was no ordinary "heretic." How does one condemn a renowned theologian
who was adored in courts and classrooms? The church
was as yet too loose in organization and doctrinal formulation to catch so big a fish; too few clerics considered Abelard a heretic. Even Bernard's reputation might
prove insufficient in the event Abelard forced a public
debate. Bernard, who seemed oblivious to the latest
advances in dialectics and scholastic theology, feared a
humiliation before the skillful Abelard who could deci-
mate the best of rhetoricians. Bernard learned about
God through private meditation and the Bible, not
through dialectic.

To make their anti-Abelard campaign more convincing, Bernard's friends reminded him that the revolutionary Arnold of Brescia (a former student of Abelard) was
in France, and that Abelard had disciples in the Roman
Curia itself. Bernard came to believe that Abelard's
teaching could undermine the whole structure of the
church. Rebels like Arnold could upset the authority of
feudal lords and bishops. The Abelardian presence in
Rome could prevent the exercise of the papal will, the
temporal side of God's will. Bernard decided to con-
front Abelard in person.

No one knows what Bernard and Abelard discussed at
their famed meeting. Apparently Abelard agreed not to
continue teaching certain doctrines. But Bernard was

evidently unsatisfied with Abelard's subsequent behavior (did Bernard realize that Abelard's disciples must also be silenced?) because he soon went to the Paris cathedral and preached to Abelard's students. Much to the annoyance of Abelard's pupils, Bernard attacked the teachings and methods of certain unnamed teachers. Abelard retaliated to this affront by publishing another edition of his book *Theology** in which he repeated his previous teachings in all essentials.

PREPARATION FOR THE COUNCIL OF SENS

At this point Bernard turned to Rome. He wrote to Innocent II accusing Abelard of the most blatant theological errors. These accusations forced Abelard, whose reputation was at stake, to approach the archbishop of Sens who promptly arranged for a public debate to be held 3 June 1140. Here, Abelard thought, he would finally clear himself of these slanderous charges. Fearing just such an open debate, Bernard at first refused to attend, but he was later persuaded that his absence might be construed as a victory for heresy. Bernard set to work soliciting supporters for his cause. He ensured that the "debate" would in fact be a tribunal in which Abelard's fate would finally be sealed.

Bernard quickly released a flood of letters to French prelates, Roman cardinals, and the pope. In these letters Bernard pronounces the untried Abelard guilty on five counts. First, Abelard is an arch-heretic. His teaching on the Trinity is Arian (Christ is not fully divine), and his doctrine of grace is Pelagian (man can be saved by his own merits).

Second, Bernard assails Abelard's character. "He argues with boys and consorts with women." Abelard persists knowingly in his error. He is a monk without a rule. He hates the faith of Christ.

Third, Abelard sees nothing "through a glass darkly" but views everything face to face. He mistakingly be-

---

*This is the *Theologia 'Scholarium'*.

lieves he can understand God's mysteries solely through reason. Nothing is sacred to Abelard who analyzes precepts of the church as if they were axioms of geometry. Bernard reminds his readers that faith is to be accepted blindly and totally. It is sinful pride to hold that God can be understood through dialectical argument, rather than through humble prayer. Faith is not some prize won by a few clever logicians, it is God's gift to all people of good will, including the simple. (But mystical faith, a special free gift of God, is of course reserved for mystics.)

Fourth, Abelard leads the "little ones" astray. He corrupts the young, and misleads the ignorant and the unlettered.

Fifth, Abelard tries to shatter the entire structure of the church. He not only imperils the orthodoxy of Catholic dogma, but he also detracts from the legitimate authority of the ecclesiastical church. As a prelate without responsibility Abelard is attempting to establish an unauthorized corps of teachers who have license to do as they please. If Arnold of Brescia is typical of his followers—the mere mention of popular revolution would make an aristocrat shudder—then God help the church! If Abelard and his band of maverick professors were to grow in influence, who would obey the pope, the bishops, and the monks? Who would obey the princes who govern at the bidding of the clergy? Soon raw and inexperienced listeners will flock to any fly-by-night heretic preacher. The unity of Christendom will be rent forever.

Bernard implies that even Abelard's specific doctrines and his contempt for the Fathers of the church will lead to the same disruptive result. If man can do without grace and has no need for redemption (the Atonement, said Abelard, was only an "example" to man), then why have the church? If Abelard permits us to receive grace directly from God, what need have we of the sacraments and the clergy who dispense those sacraments? If logicians presume to obtain their secret knowledge immediately from above (with no need of the clergy's sacraments and preaching), are they not placing themselves beyond the church's jurisdiction? If sin is not "objective" (certain acts are sinful in themselves) and only intentional, will not Christians begin deciding for themselves what is sinful and not sinful? Will they not deny the need for Penance? Abelard will reduce the objective content of Revelation (and the objective effects of the Atonement) to a mere subjective state in each individual Christian. Surely Abelard's nominalism will further encourage this kind of subjective individualism and thereby empty the church of "real" substance. The church will dissolve into an aggregate of atoms which recognize no authority above themselves.

The proper "spiritual" leaders in society, Bernard insists, are found in the monasteries, especially Cistercian ones. Abelard would upset this balance by placing this leadership role in the hands of the professors in the schools. What made Bernard's letters so effective was that his readers saw their own positions threatened by the various antiauthoritarian forces around them: antisacerdotal theories such as Donatism, popular revolts, growth of princely power, new towns, mental dislocation caused by rapid change. Bernard implies that Abelard alone is responsible for all these pressures on traditional systems of authority. Once Abelard was whisked from public life the church of old would return. To condemn Abelard, the cardinals and bishops were in effect being told, was to reinforce the power of the Roman church and the episcopal institutions.

COUNCIL OF SENS 1140

When the time for the encounter at Sens arrived Bernard was well prepared. He brought with him the archbishop of Reims and other bishops favorable to his cause. Still fearing an unobstructed discussion of Abelard's teachings Bernard arranged a meeting of the bishops the day before the council. Bernard presented them with a list of statements lifted from Abelard's books, and he apparently got the prelates to agree that these passages were heretical. By these tactics Bernard had effectively made himself the prosecutor at an inquisition. An impartial hearing was now impossible.

The next day, 3 June 1140*, a great procession filed into the cathedral. The presence of King Louis and Theobald, Count of Champagne, indicated that a political joust between the leading lay lords and certain prelates was in the making. The king and the count, both sometime patrons of Abelard, saw in Bernard a threat to their ancient right of interference in episcopal elections. Many powerful lords, lay and cleric, would certainly try to use the heresy-hunting abbot to their own less-than-spiritual ends; similarly many could make political hay out of Abelard's defense. Abelard's orthodoxy was not uppermost in the minds of those present that day. Once the proceedings commenced, Bernard seized the initiative by reading aloud propositions from Abelard's *Theology*, propositions which Abelard was expected to acknowledge. Bernard asked Abelard if they were his words. Convinced that this sham debate was but a heresy trial, Abelard refused to reply to Bernard's charges. Instead, he appealed to Rome and walked out of the church, much to the disappointment of his followers who were anxious for a rousing defense.

Frustrated at this surprise move, Bernard denounced the appeal as uncanonical and persuaded the bishops to condemn, in Abelard's absence, nineteen of the propositions. Since only the pope could now declare the person of Abelard heretical, Bernard sent the bishops' condemnation to Innocent II with a cover letter in which he reminded the pope of his duty to suppress heresy.

*The date is a matter of dispute. Some scholars contend that the council was in 1141.

To speed up the papal decision Bernard immediately wrote to several Roman cardinals and repeated the charges made in previous letters. Not surprisingly, Innocent, with indecent haste, rendered a verdict of guilty. On his journey to Rome Abelard received the bad news at Cluny where he had stopped due to his failing health. Abelard answered the pope's judgment with an assertion of his innocence; he had no harsh word for Bernard. In 1142 Abelard died in a priory near Cluny. The abbot of Cluny thereupon dispatched a letter to Abbess Heloise informing her of the death of her husband. Tenderly the compassionate abbot assured her that she and Abelard would be reunited in eternity.

If the Abelard episode were studied in isolation from the rest of Bernard's writings and activity, the abbot of Clairvaux would seem a bigoted maniac who resorted to any available means in his campaigns to crush his opponents. But Bernard's sincerity is made evident by the consistency with which he pursued the same ideals throughout his life. Admittedly some personal antagonism towards Abelard might have refracted Bernard's vision, but his overriding motive was to rid the church of God's antagonist. If on occasion he appeared unrestrained in his methods, it was only because Bernard at times had difficulty seeing the individual person who represented (for Bernard) evil forces at work. No student can ponder Bernard's *The Love of God* and his sermons on the Song of Songs, both landmarks in Western mystical writing, without coming away impressed with the author's intense commitment to the Christian life. Bernard's letters, addressed to persons of every rank, reveal his compassion for the problems of particular men and women. Many sought his advice throughout his active years. When part of the Holy Land fell to the Muslims in 1144 Bernard preached and organized the Second Crusade. In 1145 Bernard got one of his protégés, the Cistercian Eugene III, elevated to the see of St Peter. He chastised Pope Eugene for becoming too involved in litigations. The pontiff, Bernard insisted, should be more attuned to the things of God. By the time Bernard died in 1153, some 300 Cistercian houses had mushroomed in Europe.

Bernard tried to salvage monasticism as a dynamic social force, while operating within the Gregorian framework of a clerical church based in the Curia. The immediate result was healthy. After Bernard's death Christians could use the saint's name to call clergymen to task for excessive involvement in temporal matters: landed wealth, interference in affairs better left to secular rulers, entrenchment of the cardinals, papal exemptions which weakened episcopal authority, popes too concerned with their Patrimony, popes and the Curia running the church like a profitable business or a family fief. But the Cistercian phenomenon soon strangled itself by refusing to adapt to the world outside the monastery walls. By 1220 an age of another kind of spirituality had arrived, that of the friars.

SIGNIFICANCE OF THE CONFLICT

As we glance back from our vantage point in the twentieth century it is evident that Bernard and Abelard had much in common. They both typified the individualism and experimentalism so prevalent in early twelfth-century Europe. They both felt untied to any fixed tradition. While Bernard seems reactionary next to Abelard at Sens, it must be remembered that Bernard's theology derived mainly from his own inner experience; he quoted Scripture often, church authorities rarely. Bernard believed he was upholding "authority" as he conceived it, whereas he actually undercut traditional ecclesiological forms by his excessive reliance on his personal communion with God. Could not someone after Bernard deduce from the latter's subjective mysticism that the church was unnecessary as an intermediary between the soul and God? Both Abelard and Bernard wanted to soften the quickened tendency to institutionalize the church. For Abelard, this meant greater freedom to examine the body of received faith and to apply it to the needs of a given society. For Bernard, this meant the presence of contemplative monks who would remind prelates of their rightful duties in the church.

So too in their respective views on church and state they could coexist. Bernard and Abelard could live with and consciously accept the Gregorian notion of the primacy of the Roman See in the church. The pope's duty was primarily spiritual. He should work actively to reform the morals of the clergy. The temporal power should stay out of the spiritual; the spiritual power should stay out of the temporal. (It is permissable, however, for popes and bishops to possess lands such as the estates and titles which were attached to their offices.) To a large degree both Bernard and Abelard accepted the status quo. Neither monk wanted structural overhauls in the existing institutions; such would follow, if necessary, from interior conversion to Christ. Abelard and Bernard wanted governments to be more diligent in performing their ordinary duty of doing justice and their extraordinary duty of protecting clerics in need. The rulers of both church and state should together seek "right order" in society.

But beyond these general principles their similarities end. For although they both argued for a new kind of leadership, they held themselves up as different kinds of examples of the new priest-teacher: Bernard the ascetic vs. Abelard the activist. The Cistercian would reform Christian society by his union with God and his "witness" to this perfect Christian life. The professor of the urban schools would rejuvenate Christian morality by giving greater intellectual satisfaction and offering a faith which is fully at home in the "secular" world. (It is a peculiar but understandable fact of history that leaders within a given movement often show more hostility towards *each other* than they do towards opponents of their movement.) Their temperaments, more than their dogmas, kept Abelard and Bernard in permanent disagreement—to the discredit of the larger movement they both represented, namely, a reasonably flexible *ecclesia*.

Herein lies the significance of the Abelard-Bernard controversy. The conflict between them destroyed the very individualism they both sought to preserve. The two greatest movements of the age—the new learning of the cathedral schools and the new piety of Citeaux—ran headlong into each other, instead of cooperating in an effective reform of the church. They wasted their energies on each other instead of on their real enemy: the tendency of a few Gregorians to subvert local authority in the church. These Gregorians exploited the widefelt need for a focal point of unity by expanding the jurisdiction of the papal Curia. Together Abelard and Bernard might have mobilized their respective movements to organize reform on a more decentralized plane.

After the official condemnation of Abelard in 1140 (a decision itself denounced by the more farseeing men at the time), the professors were more susceptible to manipulation by popes and kings. To be sure a fair amount of academic freedom in the schools continued throughout the middle ages. But princes secular and spiritual were less prone to recognize the semiautonomy of the professor's status. The professors were always on the defensive and rarely could act independently on the larger society. From a doctrinal standpoint the scholars had to be more careful in their teaching lest they be branded as dissenters (heretics). Abelard was never canonized a saint as was Bernard. Indeed, after 1140 it was imprudent to quote from Abelard's books.

Note that Bernard got the *pope* to condemn Abelard. Bernard's reliance on the pope—and vice versa—enhanced the prestige of the papacy. Nothing since the first crusade had so ennobled the See of St Peter. Following Bernard's tinkering in European politics the popes were much more in control of their own destiny.

Finally, the fearful wrath of Bernard led, paradoxical-
ly, to a fear of mystics and to an official distrust of all
critics of church wealth. Hereafter those who claimed to
be prophets of God were apt to be considered suspect
by the soft-living cardinals in Rome. It is no coincidence
that heresy in Europe multiplied in the late twelfth century and that virtually all these unorthodox movements
preached the *poverty* of Jesus—a reaction to the growing
worldliness of the higher clergy.

CONCLUSION

From this survey of the Bernard-Abelard drama three
conclusions stand out. First, the church was at last free.
The clergy was now aware of itself as a separate order
within the total church, and was released from the
clutches of lay dominance.

Second, the Gregorian idea of papal supremacy within the church was generally accepted by Europe. The
pope, the recognized leader of the entire clergy, was the
head of a centralized organization which had sole jurisdiction in matters pertaining to the faith of Jesus.

Third, now that the clerical church had attained its
independence, should it not consolidate those gains by
increasing its power in the secular realm? That tragic
figure, St Bernard of Clairvaux, spurred on that which
he dreaded most: a papalized church propped up by an
army of bureaucrats, decretals, and even soldiers. Unwittingly Bernard opened the path for absolute papal monarchy.

The next stage in the development of church-state
relations is the church's drive to control the state.

Thy Kingdom come, Thy Will be done, on earth as it is in heaven.

III

POPE INNOCENT III AND FRANCIS OF ASSISI

During the latter half of the twelfth century the popes became embroiled with the Holy Roman Empire. In their fierce attempt to protect the Papal States the popes were further drawn into the mire of European politics. The pontiffs during this crucial period persuaded themselves that the fortunes of the Catholic church were in direct ratio to their ability to maintain the autonomy of the Patrimony and to provide strong political leadership in a chaotic Italy. To attain these ends

Pope Alexander III (1159-81), a brilliant law professor from the university of Bologna, sought to strengthen the papal government by expanding the judicial machinery of the Curia. In this way he hoped to build a solid fortress against the Italian pretentions of the German emperors.

But the centralizing tendency of the church was due not only to the personal policies of popes and their cardinals; it was driven along by the general expansion which was felt throughout Christendom. Fundamental to all twelfth-century movements were the population boom, increased industrial and agricultural production, and the fast flow of local and long distance trade. Italy in particular experienced a spectacular increase in wealth and population. The intense economic competition among Italian cities inclined them to cast about for outside protectors and arbiters. Both pontiffs and emperors exploited the mutual jealousies among the towns as well as the domestic tensions within each of them. It was natural that the papacy would attempt to rationalize its governmental structures to keep up with the changing times.

The recovery of the Roman law and the development of law schools in the twelfth century were not the inventions of ivory tower intellectuals. Rather, the return of a systematic single law (feudal law was too diverse and too rooted in a somewhat outmoded social system) was a response to the demand of governments, both secular and ecclesiastical, for an efficient administration capable of formulating and executing policy. The papacy even set up special schools where fresh law school graduates could come to receive training prior to entering the Roman bureaucracy. Since the popes were pressured to hear more and more cases on everything from disputed episcopal elections to mass liturgies, they had to develop an efficient system to handle this work load.

The cathedral school movement, of which Abelard was a part, matured in the late twelfth and early thirteenth centuries in the form of "universities," a system which still exists. In addition to the march forward in legal thought the period 1140-1270 is almost unparalleled in Western history for its advances in Latin and vernacular literature, historiography, theology, philosophy, and the visual arts. This was the age of scholasticism and wandering scholars. Architects and sculptors coordinated their bold experiments; much of this art, called romanesque and gothic, still adorns the cities and countryside of Europe. Only the later Italian Renaissance can equal the sheer quantity and high quality of artistic achievement during this time span. Amazingly, these creative activities, despite their diversity, appear to revolve around a single idea: the Kingdom of God. Many thinkers attempted to express their desire to realize this Kingdom (whether aesthetically, philosophically, legally, or politically) by ordering all reality around a common design, a mirror of the Reality of Heaven. Although working independently of each other, they all hoped that their efforts would serve to demonstrate God's operation in the world. The divine and the human would unite in such a way as to glorify both man and his Creator. They wanted not to bypass or reject man and other creatures, but rather to praise God *through* His creation. It is this overriding idea which gives some coherence to the multiple strands of high medieval culture.

But such a lofty view was shared by only a tiny minority. These confident individuals felt they had to persuade their less perceptive brethren to accept this notion of a basic unity inherent in Christendom. Educated persons increasingly sought ways to harmonize their expressions. A gothic cathedral is not simply a place to worship or a beautiful building; it is a statement of hope. The cathedral is the monarchical concept in stone. God, the supreme Monarch, seeks to restore His children to His love.

It is no coincidence that the height of the papal monarchy occurred during the creative era 1140-1270. The papacy, in part a Roman leftover of the idea of a universal order, became the symbol of this widespread quest for unity. After the eclipse of the Holy Roman Emperor as a universal fulcrum, the pope, the single most progressive force in Christendom, provided vital spiritual leadership. The centralized bureaucracy of the Holy See was the *political* expression of Europe's need for a focal point. All civilized peoples require some tangible expression of their most deeply felt values; civilization by definition implies direction. As it happened, lay politicians and clerics would forget that having once set up a universal protector they risked turning their watchdog into a police dog. Once papal institutions (as distinct from the individual holders of the papal office) were secure, no one, not even the pope, could keep them in leash.

HERESY

A problem which particularly concerned popes in the late twelfth century was heresy. It is a truism that wherever you have orthodoxy you have heresy. How can you have dissent unless you have something to dissent from? In the decades following Abelard's condemnation there was a concerted effort to define the doctrines of the Catholic faith and cast them into scholastic language. Christians agreed that Jesus taught but one gospel and that the church's job was to defend and disseminate this message. But the triple forces of scholasticism, papal monarchy, and the natural systematizing thrust found in any civilized society served to regulate the good news of love. God's love came to be spelled out in precise rules and jurisdictions. Moreover, the interpretation of Christian truth was placed firmly in the hands of the higher clergy—par excellence of the pope. Not only did the

Roman church take the initiative in the definition of dogma, but it also sought to standardize religious practices: sacramental rites, divine office for religious orders, processions, rules for religious houses. In 1100 there was a considerable degree of flexibility and variation in liturgical forms, religious practices, and theological opinion. By 1200 rites and dogma were being more noticeably shaped into a common mold.

The chief reason, then, for the spread of heresy in the twelfth century was the clerical tendency, spearheaded in Rome, to weave the multiplicity of Christian traditions into an established orthodoxy. The birth of more scientific approaches to the Bible and theology also speeded up this rush towards conformity. The risk of being stigmatized a heretic was thereby increased. But equally important for the rise of dissent was the social dislocation caused by *urban expansion* and political anarchy. Those most affected by these rapid changes were susceptible to new ideas, especially millennial prophecies forecasting the end of the world. In the cities there were too few priests available. The urban ecclesiastical institutions were designed in a simpler age and were never meant to operate in large municipalities. Far too many bishops were more interested in accruing power and wealth for their families than in educating their canons and parish priests for their spiritual tasks. In an age still a bit suspicious of material things the "worldly" lives of many priests seemed a scandal. The avaricious and lecherous cleric, always a convenient scapegoat for anything that went wrong, became a stock theme in contemporary satiric literature. Finally, the centralizing tendencies within large principalities throughout Europe frequently rent the social fabric which previously held together smaller political units.

For people religiously inclined, a more positive alternative to criticizing the clergy was to form small communes, with or without episcopal approval. While most of these groups accepted the sacramental teaching of the church, others chose to ignore priests and sacraments. Some experimented with weird forms of witchcraft and devil worship. Self-appointed ministers appeared every-where. The simple ascetic lives of these itinerant preach-ers stood in contrast to the luxury of the bishops and the complacency of the local padres. Almost all of these newly-found communes taught the poverty of Christ and the need to return to the original gospel—stripped of accretions and compromises allegedly accumulated since Jesus left the earth.

The orthodox clergy were perplexed as to the cause of this heresy. They could not agree on the nature of heresy, the proper procedure in trying heretics, or the punishment for the guilty. A few realized that the cur-rent religious revival was seeking an outlet for starved aspirations. What was needed were better priests to set a positive example. The growing centralization of the church was having the result of involving the clergy in more politics and landed wealth. But clerics who saw the problem in these terms were rare. The more typical reaction of clerics was to do nothing—or to resort to repression. Bewildered bishops passed the buck to local lay lords or to the Roman Curia. They were slow to realize that the growth of heresy could under-mine the whole sacramental system and the spiritual dominance (and political influence) of the clergy. It was difficult for bishops or abbots to have compassion for the urban poor because they themselves were usually of the noble class. Hence heresy was for them a form of *social* unrest and political revolution. They were more frightened of raggedy, red-eyed preachers than of armed troops. The preacher was for churchmen a rabble rouser who would encourage the "ungrateful" lower classes, a potent element in urban politics, to rise up against their rightful masters. The movement towards Christian unity (in doctrine, religious practices, organization) was enhanced by this clerical reaction to dissent.

In short, the clergy had become settled in the world. No longer were bishops and monks generally "outsiders" exhorting laymen to improve the state of their souls. On the contrary, these comfortable shepherds of souls now had a vested interest in maintaining the status quo. They failed to see that the wandering preachers were simply the latest example of the traditional prophetic thrust in the church calling for spiritual regeneration. The tragedy was that many of these "heretics," who sincerely desired to improve their lives and their beloved church from the inside, soon found themselves driven into unorthodoxy by overly provincial prelates. Would the clerical church miss this opportunity to utilize the dissenters' creative energy in the service of the whole church?

ITALY IN 1198

Emperor Henry VI, son of Frederick Barbarossa, appeared to be well on the way to conquering all of Italy. This boy wonder had pretensions to take not only Sicily, but the Byzantine Empire as well! One of the great might-have-beens of history, Henry VI died suddenly at the age of 33. Following his death an anti-German wave swept Italy north to south. Fortunately for these dissidents, Henry's son and heir, Frederick (the future Frederick II), was a baby of three. Thus some Italian towns wasted no time in expelling the soldiers and officials appointed by the late emperor.

Partly as a result of Pope Alexander III's impotent successors on the throne of Peter, Rome and the Papal States were slipping from the papal grasp. The prefect of Rome, an appointee of Henry VI and a representative of the emperor, pursued policies independent of the papacy. But the great noble families of Rome—Conti, Pierleoni, Frangipani, Colonna, Orsini—tried to ignore the prefect and follow a more pragmatic course. Each of the five families barricaded itself behind its own fortressed enclave within the city walls.

When the Carolingians created the Papal States in the eighth century no one could have foreseen how these lands could possibly become a liability to the papacy. At the time the Patrimony acted like a buffer from Lombard and Byzantine threats. Like it or not, later popes, especially the reformist types, were tied to this millstone which carried with it certain distasteful obligations. Once the papacy became psychologically, politically, and financially dependent on the Patrimony, it became impossible to remain neutral in international politics. When the pope jumped into European waters to rescue "his" Patrimony, the latter pulled him under. But to twelfth-century popes the issue was clear: protect the Patrimony at all costs, lest the emperor and the Italian (and Roman) factions reduce the papacy to a tractable subject. The holy office created by Christ himself for the salvation of mankind would be but a tool employed for base ends.

In 1197 the Marches, Spoleto, and Romagna were ruled by Henry VI's henchmen. Conditions in Tuscany, Lombardy, and Sicily were unstable, but even these regions appeared to lean towards the emperor. If the emperor controlled Lombardy and Sicily the Patrimony would quickly succumb to German rule. The pope's trump card, if only he could use it, was to exploit the rising tide of anti-German feeling and the mutual jealousies among and within the Italian communes. Following Henry VI's removal from the scene, it was possible for a forceful pope to seize the initiative by leading the xenophobic resistance in Italy, and in the process regaining papal control of the Temporal Power.

INNOCENT III (1198-1216)

Into this political mess stepped Innocent III, the greatest of the medieval popes. His reign of eighteen years marks the zenith of the papal monarchy. Pope Innocent III, the embodiment of the Gregorian ideal, not only liberated the clergy from lay control, he openly interfered in European politics whenever "spiritual matters" were involved. Unlike the situation in 1050, the secular state in 1200 was clearly on the defensive. In church law there was now one set of rules for clerics, another for laymen. As Christ's lieutenant, the pope instructed his clergy, a privileged class, who in turn were responsible for the souls of the laity. On paper, a neat and tidy ideal.

This is not to imply that Innocent III acquired more power over the European clergy than any other pope. Indeed, the pontiffs of the fourteenth century possessed far more theoretical and actual power over the church than did Innocent. By "Gregorian ideal" is here meant the pope's universal authority in Christendom. Innocent was the supreme arbiter who from his throne peered down upon the entire church to ensure that God's law was not thwarted. When a dispute in the church arose, the pope, as the supreme judge, presumed to know the content of God's will, and settled the matter accordingly. Sometimes Innocent took the initiative in seeking out the truth of a dispute, but most of the time he waited for legal appeals to be filed in Rome. As Innocent saw it, church and state normally operated within their own separate spheres. His job was to oversee their operations to make certain that legitimate custom was followed. He not only performed the negative function of redressing grievances, but he assumed the awesome responsibility of bringing the whole world to Christ.

Innocent III was the last universalist pope. Only he had the will and the de facto authority to behave as a true head of all Christendom. Innocent maintained a delicate balance between church and state—to the benefit of both. The Kingdom of God on earth seemed imminent. The romantic enthusiasm so characteristic of medieval psychology was perfectly reflected in this heroic pope. Europe had found its symbol to replace the imperialist universalism of Caesar Augustus. Surely Europe would now continue to fulfill its divine destiny under the papal flag.

EARLY CAREER

Innocent III was born Lothar of Segni (later to be called Conti) in about 1160. The Conti, a powerful noble Roman family, decided that Lothar would be trained for a high position in the church. After studying in Rome as a boy, Lothar continued his education in Paris where he met many of Abelard's former pupils. Later Lothar as pope would grant church benefices to his Paris teachers. From France he went to Bologna, Europe's foremost law school, for his training in civil and canon law. In 1190 Pope Clement III, his uncle, made him a cardinal although he was not yet a priest. But when Pope Celestine III (1191-1197), a member of the Orsini family which was an enemy of the Conti, became the next successor of St Peter, Lothar found himself among the unemployed.

During these years (1191-1197) of partial exile Lothar wrote in his idle moments. Among his books, all of which are rather conventional, the *On the Misery of the Human Condition* accurately reflects his pessimistic view of human nature. Throughout his life he would demonstrate his distrust of public men, preferring to place his faith in organizational structures. What the church needed, he mused, was forceful leadership at the top, together with the institutional mechanism to carry out the commands of the Roman church.

When the senile Celestine III died at the age of 92, the cardinals looked for a politically-minded candidate who could restore order and protect their family possessions from the German occupation. Their choice fell upon Lothar, a man who had few enemies and was loved by the Roman people. Lothar, at 37 the youngest of the cardinals, adopted the name Innocent III. Was Lothar inspired by the example of Innocent II who with the help of St Bernard healed the church's schismatic wounds?

Innocent III's consecration sermon, a sort of acceptance speech, reveals his exalted sense of the pontifical office.

"Who am I and of what lineage that I should take my place above kings? For to me it is said in the Prophets, 'I have this day set thee over nations and over kingdoms, to root out and pull down, and to destroy, and to throw down, to build and to plant'. To me it is said in the Apostles, 'I will give unto thee the keys of the kingdom of heaven; and whatsoever thou shalt bind on earth shall be bound in heaven: and whatsoever thou shalt loose on earth shall be loosed in heaven'. The successor of Peter is the *Vicar of Christ:* he had been established as a *mediator between God and man*, below God but beyond man; less than God but *more than man; who shall judge all and be judged by no one.*" [Italics added]

This sermon contains little of St Bernard's vision of the ascetic pope who inspires Christians by pious example. For Innocent the papal crosier was a club to be used to beat the disobedient into submission. Although supremely confident, Innocent had a crisis mentality which tended to exaggerate the dangers in certain situations. Unwittingly, some of the measures he adopted to meet specific emergencies had the unforeseen result of setting precedents for the future misuse of papal power in the church and the state.

His sermon finished, Innocent III lost no time in taking the offensive against injustice. He threw out of the papal kitchen the money changers who were charging visitors a fee before being allowed an audience with the pope. Innocent reorganized the chancery, regulated the proctors, established special agencies to handle curial business. While he would not hear every court case appealed to Rome he was quick to compensate injured persons, down to the most humble parish priest. He

created institutions which would prevent a recurrence of
persistent vices, e.g., simony.

Innocent made the prefect of Rome a liege vassal of
the papacy, and reduced the number of Roman senators
to one—to be appointed by the pope. In the short run
Innocent's aggressiveness in curbing the five families
worsened the anarchy. In 1203 the factions ran him out
of Rome but soon recalled him; they momentarily forgot that the tourist trade (VIP's, pilgrims, litigants, merchants) required the presence of the pope and his Curia.
Eventually Innocent's diplomatic skill and persistence
brought peace to a city weary of turmoil.

In the Papal States Innocent was almost as successful.
He recovered much of the Patrimony and established
the boundaries which would outlast the middle ages. A
solid political bloc in central Italy, directly ruled by the
pope, would enable him to ward off pressure from Lombardy and Sicily. But many independent-minded communes in the Patrimony, much to Innocent's annoyance, saw this arrangement as a marriage of convenience;
they defied the pope whenever they felt it was in their
interest to do so. Tuscan cities formed an anti-imperial
league, but they never came under Innocent's sovereignty although his influence in Tuscany was not slight.

Innocent headed off a Hohenstaufen union of Sicily
and Lombardy, which would encircle the Patrimony, by
getting the Empress Constance, wife of the late Henry
VI, to hand over Sicily to the pope as a fief. In her
surprise submission Constance acted not out of any
sense of loyalty to the see of Peter, but out of sound
political calculation. As regent for her three-year-old son
Constance realized that her native Normans had had
enough of German rule and she needed outside protection for her son against the Germans. Innocent drove a
hard bargain. Not only did he receive guardianship over
her son, but he assumed virtual control of the Sicilian
church. The pope was permitted to receive any appeal,
and he could "review" all episcopal elections. When

Constance died a few months later in November 1198, Innocent began his struggle for Sicily.

The trouble began when one of Henry VI's former lieutenants, Markwald, recently chased out of the Papal States, entered Sicily with a large army in 1199. When it became clear that Markwald intended to take over the regency, Innocent raised an army (which he could do legally as the temporal head of the Patrimony) and marched towards Sicily to crush Markwald. To complicate matters, one of the pope's key officials, Walter the Chancellor, also had an eye on the throne. To head off this possibility Innocent sent in another Walter, a swashbuckling French count who attracted Italians to his cause, among them one starry-eyed young bourgeois, Francis of Assisi. Innocent frantically maneuvered to regain control of the growing anarchy in Sicily. Much to his relief the would-be kings died. In 1208 after a decade of civil war and tiresome diplomacy, Frederick attained his majority. The pope was at last the master of Sicily.

HOLY ROMAN EMPEROR

All of Innocent's efforts to neutralize Sicily would come to nought if the emperor ruled both Germany and Sicily. The problem was simplified for Innocent when *two* candidates appeared in 1198, each claiming to be the rightful successor of Henry VI. Most of Germany came out for Philip of Swabia, brother of the late Hohenstaufen Henry VI. The Hohenstaufen family dominated southern Germany. These pro-Hohenstaufen elements passed over the claim of young Frederick, the rightful heir as son of Henry VI, since they feared that a non-Hohenstaufen family would steal the regency from them. In this grave situation they decided to crown Philip immediately and worry about Frederick later. The other candidate, Otto of Brunswick, was supported by north German princes as well as by his uncle, the

king of England. Automatically the king of France
declared for Philip; anyone who was anti-English could
not be all bad. Thus the German succession question
became an international affair.

Innocent was in a dilemma. He preferred not to
recognize Philip since a Hohenstaufen takeover of Sicily
would probably follow. But if he came out for Otto,
described by one chronicler as "arrogant and stupid," it
would appear that the papacy was playing politics.
Besides, Innocent wanted sworn assurances from Otto
that as emperor he would keep out of Sicily and central
Italy. Innocent bided his time while the flame of civil
war in Germany grew hotter. After a pitiable performance on the battlefield Otto's only recourse was to
submit to the pope. In 1202, the jubilant Innocent
wrangled from Otto a promise to recognize the papal
claims in Tuscany, central Italy, and Sicily.

As expected, Philip and his allies, which included
many German bishops and princes, protested that Innocent was meddling in purely temporal affairs. The
pope's job, they insisted, was simply to ratify the election of the princes. Princes not popes made emperors.
Innocent's carefully worded responses to this charge
remain landmarks in the evolution of papal theory on
church and state. In trying to justify his choice, Innocent claims that the empire really belongs to the papacy
because it was a pope (Leo III) who took the imperial
title away from the Byzantines and gave it to the Germans (Charlemagne). That is why emperors in the past
have come to Rome to be consecrated by the pope.
Therefore, the pope has the right and duty to judge the
"fitness" of a candidate. Surely a pope cannot crown a
heretic, an idiot, or a fornicator. After all, the princes'
right of election was originally given to the princes as a
concession by a pope; the princes cannot claim an inherent right to elect. When the princes make a bad choice
the pope has the duty to reject the candidate. Hence the
pope is within his rights when he turns down the claims

of Frederick (unfit because of his young age) and Philip (unfit because of irregularities in his election). Otto is the obvious choice. His electors showed "greater wisdom," and his election was "proper." Otto himself is a good Catholic and his family has always been kind to the church.

Innocent's fancy legal footwork made Otto happy but did nothing to halt the civil war, which increasingly favored Philip. In 1207 the realist Innocent was on the verge of abandoning his protégé Otto whose military cause seemed hopeless. But by a sudden "judgment of God" in 1208, Philip was murdered. The following year Innocent crowned Otto as emperor. But, alas, no sooner was the chrism dry on his royal head than did Otto break his oath and march his armies into Italy. In despair, Innocent excommunicated Otto and had him replaced by the teenage Frederick who promised not to unite Germany and Sicily. These promises were getting to be something of a habit. After seventeen years of involvement in German affairs, Innocent seemed to have finally attained full control of the imperial title. But German unity, what was left of it, was shattered. Only the great German princes emerged with increased authority.

Note that Innocent did not claim to exercise direct temporal rule in all secular states. Rather he claimed that the empire bore a *special* relation to the holy see due to previous papal policy and the Donation of Constantine. Innocent never said that he himself was the lord of the world in all spiritual and temporal matters. Despite Hohenstaufen propaganda to the contrary, Innocent sought no gain in Germany. His interference was conditioned by his desire to free the Papal States, reform the church, and launch a crusade to the Holy Land.

The German affair did nothing for the church and the papacy in the long run. Innocent angered German (pro-Hohenstaufen) bishops by interfering in their ecclesiati-

cal concerns. He alienated Hohenstaufen princes by
rejecting their elected king. According to German prelates and princes, Innocent was using his holy office for
political advantage; he was hiding behind a legal smoke
screen to conceal his worldly ambitions. Even non-
Germans became cynical about Innocent's imperial policy. It was obvious that Innocent's policies toward
England, France, and Italian communes were influenced
by his desire to gain support for his imperial candidate.
The whole embarrassing business was a portent of the
day when the papacy's credibility gap would nearly
destroy its claim to universality. Martin Luther's reformation had a captive audience in a Germany where
popes had a long history of meddling.

CRUSADE

From the minute Innocent III sat in his papal chair in
1198 he enthusiastically supported the crusade. He
dreamed of Urban II leading a mighty army of saints to
retake the Holy Land from the infidel. From 1096 to
1198 is only a century but it was enough time for a
nostalgic legend about the First Crusade to become
established. At the call of Pope Urban and the Holy
Spirit, the story went, Christians everywhere overcame
their selfish interests and rose up as one in defense of
the Lord. If only a similar venture, thought Innocent,
could recur in modern times, the divisions within Christendom would heal up and Love would reign. The gray
area between right and wrong would disappear; Christians, as in a previous golden age, would be able to
distinguish Good from Evil at a glance. The prestige of
the papacy would be restored to its true place of honor.
Today, Innocent felt, people are confused and have no
respect for authority and tradition.

The crusade concept reveals Innocent III's strongest
and weakest sides. The dream of a successful crusade
infused his rule with a selfless idealism which transcend-

ed immediate political problems. Innocent's imagination, spontaneity, and magnanimity contrast sharply with subsequent lawyer popes. The crusade model shored up Innodent's intent to keep above petty sectional disputes and to pass judgment in the interest of the common good of all peoples. The crusade was for him a means to facilitate church reform. But was the crusade ideal the most appropriate vehicle for unity in the early thirteenth century? Innocent should have realized that the crusade was at best a bore for the lay and ecclesiastical practitioners of the New Politics. The new politicians tried to combine the latest administrative techniques with the older feudal, more personal methods of organization. They were interested in constructing efficient political and financial institutions with the help of lawyers trained in the revived Roman law. A military venture to the Holy Land seemed a pointless distraction to businessmen, educated officials, and higher nobles. Innocent tried to bully statesmen into supporting an ideal which appealed largely to petty nobles, the human refuse caught in the growing centralization within both church and state government. Was Innocent so naive as to believe that the increasingly anachronistic idea of crusade would revitalize the church? Would not the idea of the holy war eventually weaken the moral authority of the clergy?

The Third Crusade (1189-1194), led by the rulers of England, France, and Germany, had failed to capture Jerusalem. The crass materialistic motives of the Italian merchants and the disgraceful behavior of France's Philip Augustus, who rushed back to France after only four months in the Holy Land to attack English lands, should have warned Innocent of the difficulty of a renewed assault. Already in 1198 Innocent sent feelers to Constantinople to sound out the prospects for Byzantine aid. The chaotic Byzantine Empire, still in schism from the West, welcomed any material help.

After many pleas Innocent finally got a few nobles from Flanders and France to lead the crusade. A deal was struck with the Venetians who were to supply ships and food for the voyage to Egypt, a convenient launching pad to the Holy Land. When the day of departure arrived in 1202 the nobles, who were never very good at logistics, discovered they had only 50,000 of the 85,000 marks they agreed to pay. The Venetians said they would fulfill their end of the bargain if the nobles would assist them in capturing along the way the Christian town of Zara, a trade rival of Venice. When Innocent heard of the seizure of Zara he promptly excommunicated all who had taken part in the attack.

After the fleet resumed its course, the Venetians announced to the crusaders that they were planning another side trip, this time to Constantinople. The Italians explained that they had to restore the exiled emperor, Alexius, to his throne before they sailed to Egypt. Some disgusted crusaders left the group and headed for Syria to fight the Muslims. The rest of the Christian army proceeded to Constantinople and, after some intrigue, took it by force. The hapless Alexius, who could not fulfill his pledges to the Latins, was murdered by an opposing Greek faction. The unpaid Western army, weary of the alleged treachery of the Greeks, then massacred the citizens and vandalized the world's most famous city. The schism between East and West was sealed by this barbarous deed. The Byzantine Empire became a Latin Empire.

The crusaders never got to the Holy Land. Instead they conquered a Christian empire. The real victors were the Venetians who had been competing economically with Byzantium for centuries. Never really interested in the crusade the Venetians unwittingly had a hand in almost annihilating one of the greatest civilizations in history. Ironically the weakening of Byzantium, which was retaken by the Greeks in 1241, paved the way for later Turkish invasions of Europe. To Europe's benefit, the Byzantine state had previously acted as a buffer zone between Islam and the West.

At first enraged by the detour, Innocent III accepted political reality. At least the East was now "reunited" with the see of St Peter. No sooner was the new Latin empire established than did Innocent resume negotiations from East to West to muster another crusade. To princes and bishops Innocent offered generous concessions to persuade them to take up the cross. He made political decisions designed to placate possible crusaders; he punished those who obstructed the effort. He arbitrated peace treaties between nations in order to free rulers for a new assault. As a last resort he summoned a general council in 1215 to reawaken the cause.

Innocent tied his fortune to the crusade; as a result both the papacy and the crusade sank in respectability. The shame of the Fourth Crusade which set Christian against Christian had to be atoned. As the instigator of this fiasco Innocent believed he had to expiate his share of the guilt by succeeding in the next crusade. But the more he met resistance to his plan the more aggressive became his requests. Innocent not only made enemies by these tactics; he made the crusade, previously a spontaneous European phenomenon, an instrument of papal policy. To support his scheme Innocent levied an unprecedented income tax on the clergy. Secular rulers would later exploit this precedent by taxing their subjects, both lay and cleric, for their own "holy" wars. Territorial wars of aggression against Christians were soon to be dubbed "crusades." In the end, Innocent's misguided crusade weakened the papacy and strengthened the secular rulers' hold over their own subjects, including their clerics.

CRUSADE AGAINST DISSENT

Characteristically Innocent III believed the supreme pontiff was chiefly responsible for guarding the purity of Christian doctrine. Since the papacy had the duty to teach the gospel, it must ensure that the gospel is not maligned by false prophets who lead the unwary to damnation. He was convinced that the episcopacy (not the state), at the instruction of Rome and in accordance with canon law, was the proper instrument for defining dogma and trying heresy cases. At the bidding of the bishops, the princes' duty was to carry out the unpleasant task of punishing the relapsed heretic.

Innocent was no fanatic in pursuing heretics. But he was swamped with complaints from legates and bishops who told hair-raising tales about long-haired preachers with strange ideas. One form of unorthodoxy appeared to Innocent particularly diabolical: Catharism. Although Innocent's career is usually associated with French Catharism, it was the Italian version which he experienced firsthand. Innocent, the born aristocrat, abhorred the spread of Catharism among the rebellious lower classes of central and northern Italy. In southern France the Cathars had even established rival churches, complete with their own "clergymen," rites, and dogma.

So concerned was Innocent with the Cathar phenomenon that he took action within a month after his election in 1198. In a letter to an archbishop in southern France Innocent commanded him to persecute the heretics and to begin an educative campaign to improve the lives of the local clergy. Innocent perceived that the spiritual laxity of the priests in that region was a partial cause of the attractiveness of Catharism. Getting no response from the bishops Innocent sent in more legates who were to prod local authorities, preach, and engage in public debates. It is a commentary on conditions in France that public debates were frequently held between Cathars and Catholics. Any self-respecting prelate would consider such a debasement of the faith a scandal. Like Bernard of Clairvaux Innocent believed the faith of Jesus was to be taught, not debated. (Can one imagine such a thing taking place in Vatican square?) It is this presumption of the Cathars to have the truth (indeed, the Cathars said *they* were the only Christians) that persuaded Innocent of the "treasonous" nature of Catharist behavior. The Cathars rebelled against the vicar of Christ who stood at the head of God's only true church; they rebelled against the divine order (Gregory VII's "right order"). At any rate, all these measures— debates, sermons, threats against nobles and bishops— failed to convert anyone.

Innocent III's exhortation to the princes shows how little he understood of Catharism and the political forces in Languedoc. For his intelligence reports he had to depend on his legates whose information was distorted due to their hatred of certain nobles in the region. Innocent III chastised Count Raymond of Toulouse, one of the more powerful nobles in Languedoc, for not exterminating heresy. But the pope should have known that any attempt by the count to suppress heresy, even if he wanted to, would spark a civil war, for many of Raymond's vassals, town subjects, and own relatives were Cathars. Anyone who persecuted Cathars would get little support in Languedoc because most people did not consider heresy a crime. Indeed, even Catholics respected Catharist leaders for their upright lives and charitable works.

The people of the southern half of the "Kingdom of the Franks" had more in common with Spaniards than they did with those of the northern part. "France" referred to either the northern half of the kingdom or the Ile de France around Paris. A businessman from Toulouse could be understood in Barcelona; he would need an interpreter in Paris. Languedoc had its own customs, laws, culture. Unlike the more feudal, agricultural North, the South, a heavily Romanized part of the ancient Roman Empire, was more urbanized and cosmopolitan. Its long trade and cultural contacts with England, Spain, Italy, and Byzantium created an exciting amalgam of East and West.

From a northern perspective Languedoc was upside down. Townspeople, serfs, and women had too much freedom. Political power was diffused among too many nobles, some of whom were better at writing love poetry than at fighting. Bishops lacked the capacity for strong political and spiritual leadership; they seemed to obey neither king nor pope. The king's feudal authority over his vassals, such as the count of Toulouse, was nominal.

Catharism was in part a residue of dualist heresies of the early church. Good and Evil vied for the souls of humans. Once Satan had persuaded Eve to commit sexual intercourse all matter became evil. Hence the sex act as well as certain foods (meat, eggs) which are the outcome of sex are sinful. Cathars claimed to have preserved the original teaching of Jesus who was a pure spirit, not a man. Since the Cathars saw no need for sacraments priests were unnecessary. They rejected hell, purgatory, relics, indulgences, marriage, oaths, war. The Cathars consisted of two groups: Perfect and Believers. Although the Perfect, a sort of priestly caste, followed a puritanical code, the obligations upon the Believers were less stringent. Unlike the male dominated Catholic clergy, women were eligible to become Perfect; this was reasonable to southerners since women, especially noble women, normally performed more important social and political functions than their northern sisters.

In 1207, the papal legate in Languedoc was assassinated. Since the legate had just excommunicated Count Raymond, Innocent assumed that the count was to blame. Innocent asked King Philip Augustus to launch a "crusade" against the Cathars; the pope promised that the "crusaders" would be released from punishment for their sins, and could retain lands taken from the heretics. Philip hesitated. How could he a feudal lord attack the lands of his own vassal? Without waiting for the king's blessing, northern nobles quickly gathered a large army and marched south to suppress God's enemies, fulfill their "crusade" obligations without the bother of going to Palestine, pick up some booty, and enjoy a good scrap. After the usual 40 days of knight service the nobles would presumably return home. All Innocent expected was a military demonstration which would pressure Raymond and other southern lords into persecuting heretics.

The military demonstration turned into a war. A petty noble, Simon de Montfort, and the papal legates made sure of that. As the barons headed home after some brief skirmishes with southern lords (the pacifist Cathars never actually did battle), Simon, in search of a principality to rule, stayed on and created an army of mercenaries. Simon's terror tactics scared the towns into submission. In 1209 Simon's soldiers entered the town of Béziers and massacred everyone: women and children, clergy and laymen, Catholic and Cathar. In his thirst for power Simon ignored the rules of combat. When he took the castle of Lavaur Simon hanged (hanging was normally reserved for lowborn criminals, never for nobles) the commander and all his knights, burned alive 400 Cathars, and threw the countess in a well which was then filled with stones. Such unchivalrous behavior shocked even northern sensitivities. As reinforcements trickled down from the North and as the southern barons quarreled among themselves Simon subdued the nobility and towns of Languedoc.

Innocent's letters to his legates reveal a man confused. The legates' reports to Rome make Raymond a demon, Simon an angel. They accuse Raymond of being soft on Catharism, hiring Jews in his government, and confiscating church lands. But Innocent personally felt Raymond was unjustly treated, and feared the growing power of Simon. What was to stop the unscrupulous Simon from exploiting the church and being his own man after the "crusade"? Innocent had tried to play one faction off against the other; as a result he lost control of the war in Languedoc. He tried unsuccessfully to halt the bloody "crusade" in order to get on with the *real* crusades against Muslims in Spain and in the Holy Land. If Innocent were to get Philip Augustus to the Holy Land he must be careful not to offend him. Philip sent his son Louis with an army to the South to make sure the new vassal, Simon, would be loyal to the crown. Innocent left the distasteful task of formally giving Raymond's lands to Simon in the hands of the Lateran Council in 1215.

After Simon died in 1218, the French king began a systematic campaign to annex Languedoc. The brutal Cathar crusade did not stamp out Catharism; the Inquisition would accomplish that. The "crusade" benefited only the Capetian kings who used the pretext of heresy to conquer the southern part of the kingdom. The invading "crusaders" from the North decimated the flourishing southern culture. The demoralized victims never fully recovered from their nightmare.

On the surface the Gregorian ideal was furthered by Innocent's control of the formerly independent Languedoc episcopacy. The papacy had shown it could get the help of the secular arm in pursuing spiritual goals. Innocent as the guardian of religious orthodoxy dealt a sharp blow to heresy.

But the papacy was the real loser. First, the expanded power of the French monarchy led to a dangerous dependency on Paris. The French king might for the moment protect the popes from the Germans, but who would protect the pope (and the French clergy) from the French king? Second, the pope's reliance on naked force in silencing dissent undermined the papacy's moral authority. Innocent played international politics like a game of chess; he was sometimes oblivious to the human suffering occasioned by war. He might have gained hegemony over the Languedoc episcopacy, but he intensified in Languedoc a deep hatred for clerics, Catholicism, and northern Franks. Throughout Europe people were finding it hard to see the gentle and forgiving Jesus sitting in the armored papal chair. After the Cathar crusade the clerical church moved faster in the direction of a tight papally-led organization which commanded obedience less by the living Word than by arms and impersonal laws.

ENGLAND AND FRANCE

The Cathar (or Albigensian) crusade became for Innocent III a sideshow which got in the way of his larger plans. While the smoke billowed in Languedoc Innocent tried to patch up a peace between the English and French kings in order to free them for the main attraction: a crusade to the Holy Land. But the search for peace was complicated by Innocent's quarrels with both monarchs.

Innocent chastised King John (1199-1216) for seizing church lands in England. The fiercest struggle was waged over the archbishopric of Cantebury; Innocent and John each put forward rival candidates. Angered at John's refusal to accept his candidate, Innocent laid an "interdict" (priests were forbidden to administer sacraments, say mass, or bury the dead) on England, an interdict which gave the English barons an excuse for revolt. After eight years of violence John not only surrendered, but he handed over the kingdom of England to Innocent as a fief, and promised to go on crusade. The barons got their Magna Carta and the pope strengthened his hold on the English church. No pope had ever intervened so blatantly in the affairs of England.

Innocent III was more circumspect with Philip Augustus because he needed the latter's support for both the Albigensian crusade and his imperial candidate in Germany. But Innocent's sense of justice sometimes triumphed over the obligations imposed by his foreign policy. In the case of Philip's maltreatment of his wife, Innocent threw aside political expediency and came down on the side of principle.

In 1193 Philip Augustus arranged a marriage to
Ingeborg of Denmark in order to have use of the Danish
fleet against England. Philip, who had never seen
Ingeborg before the wedding, ordered her back to Denmark the day after the marriage; apparently the portrait
of Ingeborg which Philip saw beforehand did not coin-
cide with the real thing. Philip had his bishops proclaim
a divorce on the flimsy pretext of consanguinity, and
married one Agnes, a Bavarian noblewoman. Eighteen-
year-old Ingeborg may not have had good looks, but she
had courage. Refusing to leave Paris she appealed to
Rome.

Recognizing the obvious justice of Ingeborg's cause
Innocent III declared an interdict on France to force
Philip to take back his rightful spouse. Despite Innocent's conciliatory attitude towards Philip in other matters—he even legitimized the bastard sons of Agnes who
herself died in 1201—the pope fought for Ingeborg until
she, a prisoner for 20 years, finally became queen of
France in 1213. It must be admitted, however, that this
victory notwithstanding, Innocent's influence in northern French affairs was perhaps less than anywhere else
in Europe. This was due partly to Innocent's interests
elsewhere, partly to the increased power of Philip
Augustus after the conquest of English lands within the
French kingdom.

ECUMENICAL COUNCIL

In 1213 Innocent III sent out legates to announce a
general council of the church. The resultant Lateran
Council in 1215 was Innocent's most spectacular
achievement. No less than 1200 bishops and abbots as
well as representatives of virtually every state in Christendom arrived in Rome. The Lateran Council, presided
over by the supreme pontiff sitting in the golden chair
of St Peter, is an apt symbol of the medieval papal
monarchy. The purpose of the council was twofold:

church reform and the crusade, the two ideals cherished by Innocent throughout his life. While his elaborate plans for the crusade, which never took place while he lived, were cautiously received by the members of the council, his reforms were of much consequence for Christian society.

The council also took up the hot political issues of the day. Innocent got the council to recognize Frederick of Hohenstaufen, who solemnly promised not to intervene in Italy, as the new Holy Roman Emperor. But Innocent had mixed feelings about the council's decision to dispossess Raymond of Toulouse in favor of Simon de Montfort. Innocent had hoped for a milder punishment of Raymond. Finally, the council condemned the radical teachings of Joachim of Flore who foretold a coming Age of Aquarius in which the Spirit of Love would rule in place of the clerical church.

The decrees deal mainly with the clergy. Innocent sought to eliminate corruption and improve the intellectual and moral standards of churchmen. All clerics including deacons are forbidden to get married, or to harbor concubines (a minority report contended that a celibate clergy only encouraged concubines, prostitution, and homosexuality). Clerics are forbidden to hunt, fight, gamble, drink excessively, practice surgery, wear loud clothes, participate in trials by combat and in ordeals by fire and water, take bribes, etc. Bishops are to assure that their priests are properly educated (quite a task since most parish priests were lowborn and unlettered), fed and housed, and attentive to their proper spiritual duties. Bishops are to make certain that marriage cases are handled only by ecclesiastical courts. No new religious order is permitted (this decree was perhaps enacted over Innocent's wishes). Jews throughout Europe are to wear a distinctive dress. Money lenders are prohibited from charging excessive interest on loans.

In matters of doctrine the most important was the decree on transubstantiation, the first formal definition of this dogma. The Real Presence of Christ in the Eucharist is spelled out in scholastic-Aristotelian terms, intelligible only to the educated. Once a year every Catholic must confess to a priest and receive the Eucharist; later this would be called Easter Duty. This last canon reveals the council's concern for the spiritual life of the laity, the first time an ecumenical council ever expressed such concern. The introduction of Easter Duty gave the clergy considerable power over the inner lives of laymen.

This tendency to separate the clergy from the laity is even more evident in the canon which permits the clergy to declare null and void any allegedly anticlerical statute passed by secular princes. This canon was probably a tactical error, for it proved impossible to enforce and only served to strain relations between church and state.

When the delegates to the council returned home Innocent probably believed that the Gregorian vision was at last near realization. To be sure, the clergy were less than perfect; the repetition of some canons enacted by previous councils proves that they were not successful in practice. But the clergy seemed to function in their own right, and were in turn subordinate to the successor of St Peter. Innocent did not invent the reformation; rather he marshaled existing reform efforts under the standard of the Roman church. The most educated and progressive people of the day cheered Innocent's efforts to eliminate injustice. Innocent the foe of particularism was a symbol of universalism; local selfish interest, which stubbornly perpetuated itself, could be overcome only by an impartial outsider. After 1215 local prelates and secular rulers continued to resist Innocent's attempts to weed out corruption mainly because they had a stake in the status quo. Yet the very existence of the Lateran Council demonstrated the near reality of a "Christendom"—unified in organization, discipline, dogma, and purpose.

One seemingly trivial incident at the council, however, was a foreboding omen. Innocent proposed a 10% flat rate income tax on all bishops to support the holy see. Typically Innocent had disadvantaged persons in mind, for these could not afford the high cost of court fees in appeals cases. Hence the Roman Curia needed additional outside revenue to keep rising court costs low. While bishops generally favored the centralization of the church, they were not willing to pay for the convenience of having an equitable arbiter. They rejected Innocent's plea. Would the papacy resist the temptation to seek alternative sources of revenue to finance its expansive bureaucracy?

PROPHECY AND ORDER

Innocent endeavored to Christianize no less than the entire church. He saw the need to keep alive the spirit of prophecy in the church by invoking a crusade, and by making "true" Christians more visible to other Christians. Hence his concern for the moral improvement of bishops and monks; he especially exhorted Cistercians to follow their rule. He knew there was a limit to what laws could do; only the pure lives of holy monks, detached from worldly cares, could inspire lax Christians to live Christ. But unlike many of his brethren in the papal palace Innocent III had the courage to admit the evident deterioration of monastic spirituality, including Cistercian. The monasteries' indecent scramble for land and money forfeited their privileged status in the church hierarchy. They seemed out of touch with the spiritual needs of the changing times. Innocent realized that alternate forms of Christian living were not necessarily heretical (as were the Cathars); these fringe groups manifested a profound unrest within the Catholic communion. This open-mindedness accounts for Innocent's confirmation of the rule of the Humiliati (the humble people), groups of poor factory workers and peasants, both men and women, who formed communist societies dedicated to the ethical teachings outlined in the New Testament. Unlike the Cathars the Humiliati requested papal approval of their rule. Innocent's delicate and compassionate treatment of the Humiliati was largely successful. Innocent wisely reasoned that it was better to have these evangelical zealots uplifting the church from within than hurling stones from without.

But most of Innocent's energy was directed at the *order* of the Kingdom. His efforts to stabilize Germany and Italy, reform clerical behavior, streamline episcopal structures, organize the financial and judicial functions of the Curia, and establish doctrinal and disciplinary conformity in the church were all intended to institutionalize the spirit of prophecy. It was clear to his contemporaries, and to Innocent in rare moments, that he was more successful in establishing law and order than in reviving Christian love. More than Gregory VII he set up an ideal of a centralized church which would guide (and plague) future popes. In practice Innocent never came close to his concept of papal monarchy, but he more than any pope since Gregory VII mapped out the course for Europe. The Kingdom of God was being realized on earth.

CONCLUSION

Innocent's glorious career is historically significant for two reasons.

First, the viable civilization of Christian Europe had fully emerged. Medieval Europe was not the late Roman Empire or the early Renaissance; it was Europe. The "middle" ages was not in the middle of anything; it was by itself. Europe *was* the Christian church (defined as the total body of Christians with their central beliefs). The clerical body with its Roman head helped to give form and direction to this thriving civilization. Europe appeared destined to be a federation of subcultures united in Christian charity. Innocent III was not a grasping despot; he was the expression of an age. Many people loved Innocent III because he showed them how to solve their problems. The clerical church was in the mainstream of European culture.

Second, the church had won its fight for liberty. With Innocent III it was the *state* which was on the defensive. He claimed that the pope was supreme in spiritual matters, the state in temporal. But in an *emergency* ("in the case of sin") the pope, who had care of the church universal, could intervene in some purely temporal concerns. While Innocent was guarded in claiming such intervention, his successors would have fewer scruples. Innocent justified his incursions into temporal politics by pointing out that the state was not sovereign; it was a department or subdivision of the church. "Church" and "state" were not separate societies; they were complementary bodies operating in unison for the perfection of man in this life and the next. The theocratic Holy Roman Emperor, spiritual son of Constantine and Charlemagne, was no longer the axis of European unity. He had been replaced by the Holy Father.

Beneath this edifice of stone was a dash of sand. Did the aggressive pope weaken the foundation of the church by trying to run everything? Were church institutions at the time mature enough to assume the responsibility of maintaining so high an ideal? Innocent made the church top heavy by moving to coordinate many prelatal and secular jurisdictions in the Lateran. A few incompetent popes could ruin the whole system. Overreacting to the dangers of heresy and disorder, Innocent tightened discipline in the ranks. But his mania for order almost drove prophecy out of the church. It took a St Francis to keep love in.

FRANCIS OF ASSISI 1182-1226

Go and sell all that you have and give to the poor and come follow me.

PHASE I: YOUTH 1182-1206

Francesco Bernardone was born about the year 1182 in Assisi, a prosperous town in central Italy. When his father, Peter, returned home from a business trip in France and saw his new son he gave him the nickname, Francesco, the Frenchman. As the child grew, Peter, a rich cloth merchant, taught him how to speak French and sing the troubadour tunes of southern France. Francis was an energetic, likeable boy who took his pleasures all too seriously. He resigned himself to the dreary prospect of someday taking over the family enterprise. But although he was dissipated Francis was not selfish. He had compassion for the beggars who lined the streets of Assisi. Sometimes he even felt guilty for being born blessed into material abundance.

The cheerful Francis was not entirely a typical boy of the urban upper classes. He found little satisfaction in his schooling, his religion, his father's business. Francis' restless spirit sought refuge from the humdrum activities of town life in fanciful daydreams. He sighed for the day when he would become a dashing knight, an unlikely possibility for a bourgeois. The more Francis listened to the Provençal minstrels who occasionally sang in the streets of Assisi, the more his imagination was enamored with thoughts of glory and knighthood. In his mind's eye, Francis relived the days of King Arthur and the Round Table, and of Roland, the perfect Christian crusader.

As the Germans withdrew from Umbria after 1197 the citizens of Assisi took up arms against their rival to the north, Perugia. Francis rushed into battle to defend his commune. When the Perugians captured several regiments and brought them back to Perugia, Francis was imprisoned with the nobles of Assisi. While others bemoaned their plight Francis was ecstatic that he had the honor of being incarcerated with veritable knights. Their coarse talk and banal conversations, however, puzzled the incurable romantic from Assisi who thought that all knights were Lancelots or Rolands.

Shortly after his release Francis at 24 again embarked in hope of military fame. This time he went to join Walter of Brienne who led Pope Innocent III's army into Sicily. Along the way Francis unthinkingly gave away his armor to a poor, unarmed knight who was also bound for Sicily. Francis returned to Assisi humiliated and dejected. How could he have passed up an opportunity of a lifetime?

Francis did not brood over this failure. He threw himself ever more earnestly into his old merrymaking. But within a few months he got bored with partying and spent long periods by himself. Since this moody behavior was uncharacteristic of the gregarious Bernardone his friends assumed he was in love. What he did not tell them was that he was undergoing a crisis of conscience. What should I do with my life? How can I become a famous prince and a cloth merchant at the same time? Unwilling to seek advice from his family or the local priest he set out on a pilgrimage to the tombs of the apostles.

When Francis arrived in Rome he dismounted at a shrine to pray. He was scandalized at the small amount of money the pilgrims offered. Suddenly he flung his entire money pouch at the tomb's grating, startling the pilgrims around him. The impulsive Francis was generous to the point of recklessness. To him, nothing justified being tightfisted to the Prince of the Apostles. A more reform-minded person might have questioned the wisdom of pilgrimages and of leaving money at a tomb.

Should not the money be put to some practical use?
Such a question would never have occurred to Francis
whose Catholicism would always remain as conventional
as the most simple peasant's.

Turning from the shrine he asked a street beggar—the
Pilgrim City was full of beggars—to swap clothes with
him for the afternoon. Dressed in rags, speaking in
broken French, Francis begged alms. At the end of the
day Francis gave the astonished beggar back his old gar-
ments and started back to Assisi. It is fitting that Francis began his strange odyssey in the Papal City. Rome
and Assisi would soon form the axis of a reformed
church.

As he neared Assisi Francis was horrified to see a
leper alongside the road. Frances always had a fear of
becoming disfigured or crippled. Whenever he encountered lepers, who begged outside the walls of Assisi, he
rushed past them without looking. But this time Francis
experienced guilt for letting his natural emotions dictate
his actions. He quickly dismounted and grabbed the
leper's rotting hand and kissed it. Galloping away sing-
ing, Francis was jubilant at his show of courage and
self-mastery.

These unusual experiences changed Francis' life.
Henceforth he was given to long periods of solitary
prayer. During one of his strolls outside Assisi Francis
stopped at the tiny dilapidated church of San Damiano.
Some years after Francis' death his followers would
write—writings still extant today—that it was in this
obscure church that Francis had a mystical experience.
As Francis stared at the wooden crucifix Christ spoke to
him: "Repair my church." With his usual literal-minded-
ness he interpreted the message to mean: repair the
walls of the church of San Damiano.

PHASE II: CONVERSION AND SEARCH (1206-1210)

When his father was out of town on business, Francis
took some fine cloths from the family store and sold

them in the neighboring town. He intended this money to be used to buy stone and timber for the reconstruction of the chapel. But the priest of San Damiano refused to accept the gift, since he had no wish to tangle with the powerful Bernardone clan. In disgust Francis threw the coins on a window sill inside the church.

When Peter Bernardone returned to find his cloth and his son missing he decided to put an end to Francis' foolishness. Peter had Francis placed in chains and locked in the cellar. After his mother released him Francis returned to San Damiano. Several more confrontations between son and father convinced the latter that only the threat of banishment would induce Francis to act more responsibly. Peter requested the town magistrates to force Francis to repay the illicit money. Not wishing to get involved in a domestic dispute, the magistrates informed Peter that the case belonged in the bishop's court since Francis claimed to be a man of religion. At the trial, Bishop Guido ordered Francis to return the money to its rightful owner. When the bishop finished his speech Francis stepped forward and faced his father. Turning towards the bishop, Francis removed his clothes and placed them along with the money before the prelate. Then facing the astonished crowd the naked defendant spoke: "Up till now I have called Peter Bernardone my father; but since I now intend to serve the Lord, I give back to him the money, about which he was so angry, and all the clothes which I have had from him, wishing to say only 'Our Father Who art in heaven' not 'my father, Peter Bernardone'. " Peter sheepishly gathered up the clothes and money as he left. Francis' dramatic gesture (reminiscent of the trial of Socrates) had turned the accuser into the accused. Bishop Guido, genuinely moved by Francis' sermonette, put a cloak around him and led him out. Francis' courtroom spectacle made it difficult for him ever to return to his former life in Assisi. While such theatrics may have been tinged with self-righteousness the symbolic act had the result of confirming him in his new vocation.

But the nature of that vocation was vague. As he left Assisi for parts unknown he imagined himself God's troubadour who sang the praises of poverty. No sooner was he outside the city than was he mugged by highway bandits and left in a ditch. Half-starved, he found work in a monastery kitchen. After the monks drove him out he returned to San Damiano.

In his previous life as a comfortable bourgeois Francis most feared losing his handsomeness, his social status, and his financial security. Thus, in order to do himself the most violence, he visited leper colonies, and worked with his hands like a lowborn manual laborer. In the streets of Assisi he begged for his daily bread and for supplies to repair churches around the commune. Some of Francis' old friends mocked him; others were saddened at seeing him so degraded. He seemed oblivious to the suffering his behavior caused his bewildered family.

On 24 February 1206 at the church of the Portiuncula Francis heard the priest recite this text during the mass:

> "As you go, preach, saying, the kingdom of heaven is at hand. Heal the sick, cleanse the lepers, raise the dead, cast out devils. Freely you have received, freely give. Provide neither gold, nor silver, nor brass for your purses, nor scrip for your journey, neither two coats, neither shoes nor a staff, for the workman is worthy of his meat."

These words struck Francis like a thunderbolt. All Francis had to do to become a knight was to take these words literally. A knight of Christ.

As Francis made the rounds supplicating food he would chat with anyone who would listen. Bubbling with enthusiasm Francis would greet passers-by with, "Peace be to you," then he would tell them about the life hereafter. Sometimes a crowd would gather to listen to Francis exhort them to follow the Man of Suffering. Francis discovered he was a gifted preacher, and the people of Assisi loved a good sermon. The native clergy's homilies—when they were given at all—were textbookish and boring. More interesting were the itinerant lay preachers such as Cathars and Humiliati who often visited the city.

Francis relished the company of humans too much to consider becoming a hermit. His free spirit would not allow him to join a monastery. Who ever heard of a knight of Christ hidden away in a cloister? God had surely reserved this troubadour for some great task. Francis the stubborn individualist was made to lead, not follow.

After some years men asked to become Francis' disciples. One of the first was Bernard da Quintavalle, a rich city magistrate. To find guidance Francis opened the gospel at random. His finger came down at: "If you will be perfect, go and sell all that you have and give to the poor." He joyfully announced to Bernard: "This is our life and rule." On that day in April 1209 Bernard went to his mansion and had all his possessions distributed in the piazza. Arm in arm Francis and Bernard left Assisi.

By the summer of 1210 Francis and his disciples, now eleven in number, were living at the Portiuncula in the manner of a religious fraternity. They worked as farm hands in the nearby fields, but Francis permitted them to accept only food as payment, never money. Whenever they were given clothes they distributed them to the poor.

Francis realized that more would probably join his troop. Some written statement setting down guidelines was needed. Besides, someone must have told Francis that lay religious communities were in constant danger of being branded heretical. Hence Francis drew up a short rule, largely selections from the gospel, and set out for Rome with his band. In Rome they were fortunate to encounter Bishop Guido of Assisi. Through his connections in the papal Curia the sympathetic bishop got

an audience arranged with the Holy Father himself.
Innocent III and Francis of Assisi stood eye to eye.
Francis asked that his rule be approved as the basis of
his new order. Without answering, Innocent retired with
his cardinals to consider the request. Innocent could not
believe that humans could survive in such extreme
poverty, as outlined in the rule. At that moment Innocent remembered a dream he had recently. In it he saw a
tattered beggar supporting with one hand the Lateran
Palace which was falling down. Could this have been a
warning from God that the church was decaying of its
own corruption and that this mendicant could save it?
No one was more convinced of the sad state of the
church than Innocent. His treatment of the Humiliati
and the Cistercians reveals his belief in the need for the
torch of absolute purity to burn in the church. This
intense Assisian, Innocent may have mused, is probably
not a heretic since he did come to me, the pope, for my
blessing. Would God ever forgive me if I ignored this
sign from heaven?

To be on the safe side Innocent, probably against the
advice of the Curia, decided to grant Francis permission
to preach, pending local episcopal approval. But he did
not accept Francis' rule. The cautious Innocent promised Francis that he would pray for him and instructed
him to return in a few years to report on his order's
progress. Innocent had the troop tonsured as a sign of
their religious status. At that, Innocent returned to
more pressing political problems. Since some of the
brethren were disappointed that Innocent gave the order
only oral confirmation, Francis had to assure them that
their mission was a success. The Twelve left Rome as a
new order within the fold of the Catholic church, firmly
tied to the see of St Peter.

PHASE III: THE GOLDEN AGE (1210-1216)

The Twelve soon found themselves back at their
beloved Portiuncula church. They continued to lead

simple lives begging, preaching, working in the fields,
helping the poor and the lepers, praying. Some were so
touched by the pure lives of these selfless men of God
that they asked to enter the group. Francis welcomed
all, no questions asked: rich or poor, noble or bourgeois,
townsman or peasant, cleric or lay. Slowly the order
grew.

A comparison of Bernard of Clairvaux with Francis of
Assisi illustrates how different the world of the thirteenth century was from that of the twelfth; Bernard
and Francis represent two different stages in the evolution of Europe.

In the first place the mixed human types in Francis'
clique contrast with the more uniform types surrounding Bernard. The generally highborn Cistercians were to
be the heavenly elite just as the landed nobility were to
be the earthly elite. One cannot imagine Bernard recruit-
ing an ignorant peasant. Bernard got a good response
among the noble class partly because the aristocratic
ethic of leadership was rooted in actual socioeconomic
conditions.

But Francis wanted his group to represent the total
society. Francis' earliest disciples reflect the universality
of his appeal. There was Bernard, the wealthy city official. Juniper was a dense fellow who bungled every job
assigned to him. When not playing games with children
Juniper was playing pranks on the brethren at the
Portiuncula. Less eccentric was John who took Francis'
command to "follow my example" so literally that he
knelt when the master knelt, coughed when the master
coughed. The timid Rufino was a solitary introvert given
to meditation. Leo was an educated priest and secretary
to Francis. The handsome Masseo was a brilliant public
orator. The learned Elias, a future General of the order,
had a first-rate legal mind and a sense of organization.
Franciscan tradition has stressed the peculiarities of
each of the earliest disciples. Francis' interpretation of
Christianity was catholic enough to embrace all of God's

children who kept the fullness of their humanity when
they entered the fraternity.

Second, Francis' attitude towards women was uncommon among founders of medieval religious orders.
Bernard's movement was for men only. The male virtues
associated with knighthood—courage, loyalty, heroic
self-sacrifice, physical and mental strength—were transferred from the castle to the cloister. Although Bernard
the nobleman could be gracious to individual women he
constantly warned his monks of female deceitfulness.
Francis, on the other hand, was never affected by this
traditional monastic hostility towards the fair sex.
Women as well as men visited the Portiuncula. The poor
man from Assisi freely mixed with both sexes of all
ages.

There are no women in the lives of St Benedict and
St Bernard. In Francis' life there was Clare, a girl with
whom he developed an intimate friendship. In 1212
when she was seventeen, Clare heard Francis preach in
the cathedral at Assisi. After repeated meetings with the
brethren at the Portiuncula Clare longed to serve Christ
in the manner of the merry beggar. Francis might have
been unconventional, but to let a young woman move in
with them would be more than public opinion could
stand. Also, the brothers feared her powerful Favorone
family. And so it was tacitly agreed that she would
adopt Francis' way of life, but not in direct conjunction
with him and his disciples. Acting in concert with the
kindly Bishop Guido, Francis had Clare's beautiful hair
cut off in a midnight ceremony at the Portiuncula to
symbolize her break with the world. The subsequent
story of Clare is complex. After some hectic years the
pope forced her and her community of nuns to accept a
Benedictine rule—contrary to the wishes of Francis.
Francis was too far ahead of his time. The official
church had little room for fervent women outside the
cloister—hence the increasing membership of women in
heretical sects throughout Europe.

Third, Francis and his disciples were not monks. While most religious orders at the time were monastic, Francis and his followers were traveling preachers, not stationary ascetics. The Portiuncula was not a monastery; it was a home base where the brethren could return for spiritual nourishment. They spent as much time in other parts of Italy as they did at Assisi. Monks owned their property in common; the brethren owned nothing, not even the Portiuncula. Francis was neither abbot nor organizer. Accustomed to acting on the spur of the moment, he never planned for the next day. He led by the power of his personality, not by virtue of any legal office he may have held. His rule was simple and flexible, far from the detailed prescriptions of the Cistercians. Monks had houses of study and scriptoria; Francis believed that education was dangerous. He considered books a luxury which violated the spirit of poverty.

Unlike the agriculturally-oriented monks of the countryside Francis' friars were urban directed. The brethren fulfilled a need too often neglected by the monks, canons, and parish priests. With Francis the Christian ethic was modernized and made relevant for the spiritually-starved townsfolk of Italy. Soon the Franciscans would sweep the whole of Europe, for they were a godsend in a society which was still aristocratic-monastic in its ethos, but increasingly bourgeois and lay in its social and political institutions. Moral standards tended to lag behind accelerated institutional change.

Fourth, Francis praised the virtue of poverty in terms that would have startled Bernard. The Italian troubadour personified it as Lady Poverty, to whom he sang chivalrous songs. Poverty was for him more than a prerequisite for sanctity; it was the fulfillment of a romantic quest. Francis' infatuation with poverty seems almost mystical. He insisted that his brethren be literally the poorest of the poor, the most despised of the world.

He called them friars minor, lowly brothers. His passionate hatred of money was legend.

Fifth, Bernard's indifference to the visible world was deemed proper for a monk in the twelfth century. It is said that the abbot, once deep in prayer, walked halfway around the beautiful Lake Geneva without even noticing it. Francis, however, reacted to his surroundings with an intensity that seems more Eastern than Western. He had no abstract idea of Nature; rather, he revered the individual creatures he encountered daily. Francis was awe-struck when he came across something as commonplace as a sparrow. It was said that he preached God's word to birds as he passed through the woods, praising their beauty and song. Francis referred to a cricket as his "sister" who would return each day to sing for the saint. He ordered the brothers to cut down trees well above the roots so they would grow again. Out of respect for Brother Fire, he refused to put out candles at night. Francis removed worms from the road, lest they be trampled. At Gubbio he tamed a ferocious wolf.

The veracity of these strange stories is less important to the historian than the fact that they were widely accepted as true. The point is that many thirteenth-century Europeans, especially weary urbanites, needed a new culture-hero to replace the monk-type who was supposed to be oblivious to the world of sense. City dwellers found it easier to identify with a Christian activist who was acutely aware of his surroundings. Gone was the ideal of the downcast ascetic who hurried through this vale of tears; enter the merry troubadour of Assisi who admired being in all its forms. To Francis, nature was not something to be exploited by man; it was part of man. Man must learn to blend into the rhythm and harmonies of his environment. To become a Christian there was no need to flee the world and one's own humanity.

The period 1210-1216 was the Franciscan Heroic Era when the gospel was supposed to have been perfectly lived. This was the time when the spirit of the primitive church, as portrayed in the New Testament, burned in the hearts of those united as one in the will of Francis. This myth of a lost golden age, akin to the legend of the Old West in America, was fabricated later by frustrated Franciscans. These "Spirituals," as the purist brethren were to be called, bitterly condemned the majority "Conventuals" for supposedly perverting Francis' pristine order. The die-hard Spirituals never lost sight of their nostalgic Age of Innocence.

In November 1215 Francis was in Rome. A meeting with the Spaniard Dominic, also the head of a band of preachers, made him wonder about the place of his own order in the total church. Just then, he received word that the Lateran Council had passed a decree banning the formation of new religious orders. But Pope Innocent III persuaded the council to accept Francis' Friars Minor, on the basis of the oral commitment he gave Francis in 1210.

The Lateran Council's decision to accept the friars was one of the most momentous decisions made by the medieval church. For by it the spirit of love was incorporated into the institutional church. If the friars of Francis and Dominic had been outlawed as heretics, as in fact had so many similar brotherhoods, the clerical church might have quickly stagnated into a closed corporation held together by laws, force, and a papal bureaucracy. Why? Because the popular other-worldly ethic, previously expressed organizationally by monks, was still required for effective leadership in the church. The Gregorian framework needed a charismatic biblical thrust to infuse it with life, and keep it in touch with the spirituality of the times. Innocent III was perceptive enough to realize that the Cistercians were ill-suited for the task. Only the friars could reunite the twin tradition of prophecy and order. But Innocent died too soon to know he was right. The friar movement linked up with the papacy; the contact released a torrent of creative energy. The thirteenth-century papacy employed the "mendicants" (beggars) to extend the judicial arm of the Roman Curia, improve the morals of the clergy, revive theology in the schools, preach the crusade, convert the heretic, staff the Inquisition.

In 1216 Francis came to realize that his overgrown family required organization. He decided that only at a general meeting could he explain his intentions to all. The order could no longer limit its efforts to the environs of Assisi; its mission was to serve the whole world. The golden age had ended.

PHASE IV: EXPANSION (1217-1223)

In 1217 Francis called the brethren together at the Portiuncula. At this chapter it was decided to send friars throughout Europe and the Holy Land. For this purpose provinces were created and ministers appointed for each. Francis, who chose France for his apostolic work, gave a parting sermon as the enthusiastic friars scattered for parts unknown.

On his way to France the little poor man stopped in Florence where he met Cardinal-Bishop Ugolino, the eminent papal legate and canon lawyer. Later to become pope (Gregory IX, 1227-41) this statesman-diplomat labored with his uncle, Innocent III, for the reform of the church. Inspired by Francis' sincerity Ugolino persuaded him to stay and preach in Italy. The cardinal warned Francis that many prelates in the papal Curia wanted the new order to be curtailed or disbanded. He convinced Francis that his presence in Italy would encourage the friars. Before leaving, Francis asked Ugolino to become their Protector at the papal court, a position soon confirmed by Rome. Thus began a warm and lasting friendship.

Ugolino never understood Francis. Though he had the best of intentions he unwittingly weakened the spiritual pillars of Francis' fraternity. The legate knew that Italian bishops resented the intrusion of the popular mendicants who were in effect performing those pastoral obligations neglected by complacent prelates. In order to permit the brothers to go about their good work unmolested, Ugolino sent letters to bishops requesting them to give the friars facilities for preaching and building. He sincerely believed he was doing Francis and his followers a good turn.

In May 1219, 5,000 friars attended a chapter held at the Portiuncula. Here organizational matters were discussed and new missions planned. Francis picked up sounds of gossip as he milled in the crowd. "Why can't we accept a steady supply of food and money so we can be freed for the more important tasks of preaching and of combatting heresy?" "We need a tough, businesslike leader who can protect us in our work from obscurantist priests, bishops, and townspeople." "We who are priests should have more say." "We scholars need books and places of study if we are to write the truth." Stung by these complaints, Francis gave a tearful sermon to the assembled brethren. He reminded them that God called him not to the Rule of Benedict or Augustine, but to *his* Rule: the simple life of the poor Christ. His homily ended, Francis appointed two vicars to act in his stead while he went to the Holy Land to convert the Muslims. This time Ugolino could not hold him back. Was Francis running away just when the order needed his guidance? Did he finally realize that his idyllic band of troubadours was slipping from his grasp? A martyr's death in the Holy Land would immortalize his undefiled hope.

By June 1219 Francis was in Egypt talking to Christian crusaders. He foretold (correctly as it turned out) that the Christians would be defeated if they attacked Damietta. Afterwards he requested permission from the papal legate to visit the Sultan. It was common for papal

legates and even Cistercian monks to accompany crusaders, much in the manner of a twentieth-century chap-
lain who gives tacit consent to his nation's godly war.
Unlike St Bernard, who gloried in "just" wars against
the infidel, Francis hated all forms of bloodshed. Since
it was psychologically impossible for the romantic Francis to abandon the crusade idea, he transformed it into a
crusade of love. Rather than kill infidels he would convert them. Surely the pious example of his friars would
induce their hardened hearts to accept the true faith.
Against all odds Francis somehow got an audience with
the Sultan. The two talked about matters religious for
several days, each impressed by the other's integrity.
Disappointed that the Sultan remained obdurate Francis
set out for Palestine to walk in the steps of the Son of
Man. The mendicant drive to convert Muslims in the
thirteenth century was to prove unsuccessful.

Meanwhile Ugolino was at work. Francis' worst
enemies were his well-meaning friends. The protector
induced Pope Honorius (1217-1227) to issue letters to
all prelates to facilitate the friars' preaching. Strict rules
concerning fasting were imposed upon the friars—
contrary to Francis' preference for flexible rules to be
applied as a brother saw fit. The realist Ugolino believed
that since mortals were incapable of the heroism lived
by the holy Francis, some rigid guidelines were necessary for the ordinary brethren. The pope also decreed a
year's probation period for any candidate seeking admis-
sion to the order.

Some of the brothers who were scandalized at these
developments hurried to the Holy Land to inform Francis. Francis boarded the next ship for Italy. On his way
to Assisi he passed through Bologna where he discovered
a house of study built by his own minister in deliberate
violation of the rule of absolute poverty. Beside himself,
Francis upbraided the minister and ordered all the
brethren out of the house, including the sick. Before
Francis could destroy the building Ugolino sent word

that the building was actually his. He had merely "lent" it to the brothers.

When Francis arrived at Assisi it was clear he was no longer in complete charge. The educated priest-friars were turning the order into an ecclesiastical army in the service of the church. In despair Francis appealed to the pope to permit Ugolino to adopt harsher measures in dealing with the false brethren. Ugolino was of two minds. For although he sympathized with and even encouraged the modernizing tendency of the organizing party within the order, he did not want to antagonize Francis. Besides, even Ugolino realized that Francis was the vital impulse which animated the whole movement. No one, least of all a canonist administrator, could replace the holy Francesco. Francis saw no way out. He abdicated. He turned the order over to Peter Catani who died shortly thereafter. In search of a firm hand Francis then appointed his old friend Elias as the new head. With this appointment the victory of the organizers (or conventuals) was assured.

By 1221 Ugolino and the organizers had convinced Francis that the Rule was vague and out-of-date. It was unthinkable that anyone but Francis should revise the Rule. In 1210 there were no provinces, ministers, houses, properties, schools, papal privileges; there was no Cardinal Protector. From twelve the order had multiplied to several thousand—including priests, scholars, former churchmen. Ugolino argued that the Rule had to be adapted to modern times if the order were to survive and be effective in reforming the church. Francis used that opportunity to reiterate his original ideals of humility and absolute poverty. In this revision of 1221, more of an appeal to his brethren than a legal formulation, he expanded on the primitive Rule of 1210 and even made a few compromises in the hope of maintaining harmony in the order. Francis submitted the document to the General Chapter for ratification, believing he had reconciled the dissident ministers while preserving the spirit of the order's early days. Having no taste for political in-fighting, he then stepped aside.

PHASE V: LAST DAYS (1223-1226)

It is not known whether or not the chapter accepted the Rule of 1221. But Pope Honorius and Cardinal Ugolino rejected it and implored Francis to write another. Convinced that the dissident ministers would draw up a rule without consulting him, he composed the Rule of 1223, still the official Rule of the Franciscan order. The Rule of 1223 is brief and legalistic. No doubt he had assistance from Elias or Ugolino in compiling it. While the Rule does forbid friars to accept money and own possessions, it compromises many of Francis' precepts, e.g., the evangelical command to carry nothing on a journey. The whole idea of following a "rule" was foreign to Francis' simple life-style. Every brother was different, and each had to imitate the Master in his own way. With the confirmation of the Rule of 1223 the relaxing party had won.

The years 1221-1224 were hard. Francis watched his fraternity lose its innocence. As the order expanded, it diluted Francis' cherished ideals of poverty, humility, and equality. He heard rumors that brothers were owning chapels and parishes, houses of study, even money. Scholar-friars were studying and writing. People would soon look up to and bow before a renowned professor-friar or powerful bishop-friar. Soon the brothers would self-righteously attack clerical abuses (as they already were), challenge Catholic dogmas, preach without episcopal permission, presume to dominate the "ordinary" people from their lofty offices in church and state. Soon the articulate *priest*-friars would feel superior to the illiterate *lay* brothers. Soon the brethren would become rich and fat; they would take their places beside the guardians of the status quo. Stop! Was not the order founded precisely to combat the religious softness prevalent in the world? Francis left home not to become famous, but to become the poorest of the poor, and the lowliest of the low (Friars Minor). He wanted to imitate the suffering Jesus, the same Jesus who was born in an animal stable. To serve the Father, Jesus had no need for learning, wealth, or special privilege. Out of love for Jesus the ignorant and despised disciple from Assisi would reject the world and depend totally on God's goodness.

Ugolino was a spiritual brother of Innocent III. They both saw religious orders as weapons to be used against corruption in the church. But the Poverello wanted to win souls for God by personal example. While others led men to God from monasteries or episcopal chairs, his way was the Cross. Shunning positions of power the order of Friars Minor was for Francis not to be a vanguard for social reform (though reform might be a by-product), but rather a body of holy individuals whose lives induced others to repentance. They were heroic Christians who aspired to return to the evangelical life of the primitive gospel. The brothers were not God's policemen who terrified God's little ones; they were prophets whose presence was sufficient to spread the good news of love. Francis preached the conversion of individuals, not the reformation of institutions.

Sometime during these final years Francis wrote a letter addressed to all rulers in the world. This letter sums up his attitude towards the secular state which, for him, existed for a moral end: to bring people to God. Princes are to arrange public prayer every evening and give collective thanks to the Almighty. They should receive the Eucharist regularly. Ignoring the role of the clergy, Francis orders his princely readers to receive his advice as a message from heaven—refusal to act on it could condemn them to hellfire.

Throughout his life Francis held a deep respect for government officials. He neither criticized them nor knowingly thwarted their wishes. He thought little of

preachers who took advantage of their popularity by
disobeying legitimate authority. Like St Bernard Francis found an awesome dignity in political office, an
office not made by human hands. But unlike the Cistercian, the friar minor did not speak condescendingly of
the "temporality" of rulership. Francis was not given to
comparisons between temporal and spiritual, lay and
clerical, prince and prelate. He did not feel that a monk
was ipso facto superior in any way to a "secular" politician.

To be sure, Francis' attitude towards the state's function was primarily spiritual. The ruler's chief instrument
should be the force of his own edifying personal life;
coercion is rarely necessary. Francis did not foresee that
his concept of rulership could be used by secular rulers
to rationalize exploitation of the clerical church.

Francis saw no reason why princes and their subjects
could not live in harmony. If both rulers and ruled were
good Catholics tension would evaporate. A truly religious ruler would govern justly; a truly religious citizen
or subject would willingly cooperate. Francis did not
distinguish between the good Christian and the good
political man. While Francis' conservative and conventional view of princely behavior could serve to elevate
governmental standards, it could also be used by political dissidents as an inducement to disobedience or rebellion. By Francis' norm a politician could be maligned
not only for incompetence or partiality in a dispute, but
even for alleged impiety, e.g., failure to attend mass.

If the above conception of secular government seems
naive and simplistic, it is because Francis had little
knowledge of practical politics and little capacity for
logical reasoning. He perceived in word-pictures and
analogies, not in consistent patterns. His intuitive mind
had little room for abstract theories.

Francis' view of the church was similarly lucid and
personalist. The church was for him the people of God;
it was primarily the individuals he met daily, in whom

he saw the Lord. The mystical Body of Christ was synonymous with the earthly church which included cleric as well as lay.

But Francis also saw the church as an institutional structure, another widespread definition of the church in the high middle ages.* He believed himself a loyal son of this *clerical* church whose teaching and ministering must not be questioned. Francis' unsophisticated faith posited a single authority with a single interpretation of Revelation. Francis insisted that the friars were to assist the church, not to work outside it.

Francis' rosy conception of church-state relations as an exercise in shared love had a threefold result for the church. First, the Franciscan respect for the clergy tended to increase the latter's authority in the church. Unwittingly, Francis gave a boost to the Gregorian notion of a priestly caste responsible for establishing moral standards for society.

Second, Francis' emphasis on the common moral goals of both prince and prelate reaffirmed the ideal of a united Christendom. Francis taught a program of love: if men could learn to love each other and, at the same time, the Lord Jesus, institutional cooperation was supposed to follow. Thus the myth of a single Christian society was assured of longevity.

Third, Francis' model of a spiritualized clergy had the tragic but inevitable result of augmenting tensions between church and state. Francis' ideal for priests was perhaps too elevated. Understandably, Christians compared the friars with the secular priests, and found the latter wanting. Secular princes delighted in the mendicant attacks on the bishops, abbots, popes, bureaucrats. Princes learned to use the clergy's "worldliness" as an additional excuse to rob the church and meddle in church affairs. As the de facto strength of the state grew

---

*Another thirteenth-century usage of "church"—occasionally utilized by canonists—was the Roman see or the papacy.

in the thirteenth century, secular lords used this power to roll back some of the economic and political might of bishops—under the pretext of reforming the church.

Though Francis himself endeavored to prevent church-state antagonisms,* his love ethic was partially responsible for creating the "problem" of church and state. Before the thirteenth century there was no "state" in Western Christendom in the sense of an autonomous governmental public power operating within a given territory, itself subject to no external political authority. But after 1200 the "state" as an idea and as a political reality was clearly emerging. Many thirteenth-century "states" are "departments" of the church, as well as independent political entities. In a small way, Francis helped to strain the social fabric within Christendom by encouraging the "church" (as the clergy) to think of itself as distinct from the "state" (as the lay public authority). The state accused the church of being too secular; the church accused the state of being too spiritual. The issues were, of course, finally settled by force of arms and in the law courts, but the disillusionment and cynicism which followed the clashes were in part the outcome of an archetype too lofty for the likes of humans.

During the years 1224-1226 the fraternity was out of Francis' hands. He spent his final days in lonely caves contemplating the divine mysteries. When the brethren could find him they took Francis to physicians in the hope of improving his failing eyesight and digestive disorders. A hot iron applied to his face in an attempt to restore his eyesight was to no avail. As Francis was transported from place to place crowds rushed to see and touch the holy man. This unsolicited popularity must have made the weary Francis smile as he recalled his yearning for glory when a young man.

---

*For example, he tried to settle the strife between Bishop Guido and the government of Assisi.

Francis returned to Assisi to die. It was probably here that he wrote his famous Testament. In this extraordinary document Francis makes one final appeal to his brethren to hold fast to his ideals, and be true to Lady Poverty. Reviewing his life, Francis relates how he worked with his hands and begged for his bread. Francis forbids his brothers to accept papal letters of privilege to obtain houses, churches, and protection from persecution. He reminds his readers that his Rule, hard though it may seem, came from God and was not derived from any other Rule. All dissidents are to be corrected by Protector Ugolino.

In October 1226 Francis died at the Portiuncula, where it all began. As he lay dying he told the brothers about the poverty of Jesus. His final request was to be placed naked on the ground outside. The man of peace had found rest.

CONCLUSION

In Francis of Assisi Innocent III found his alterego. Innocent was the church's body, Francis the soul. What the pontiff established in institutions and legalism, the beggar complemented in pure love. Innocent realized that the full-blown Gregorian church, with its canon law and its diplomatic and administrative machinery, required an ascetic core if it were to materialize. While Innocent lived, the papacy's attempts to unite prophecy and order failed because it relied too much on organizational muscle. It was not until after his death that the fire of charisma, in the person of Francis, ignited the clerical church. The church had at last cornered the otherworldly tradition of heroic individualism, person-to-person love, pentacostal spontaneity, and the primitive spirit of the apostolic church. The Gregorian millennium seemed to have arrived.

In a sense, Bernard and Abelard were "outsiders" who brushed with the official episcopacy only when they had to protect their own interests. Pope Innocent III was an "insider" who wisely invited Francis to join him within the church. Francis narrowly missed being shut out as a heretic. As it happened, the papacy and the friars united to trigger the creative burst that rocked thirteenth-century society. It is no coincidence that many of the towering geniuses in that century were mendicants.

Glancing back over the period 1050-1226 three things are evident. In the first place, the First Revolution is over. The Gregorian revolution, so radical in 1075, has become the Establishment. Most of Gregory VII's principles are taken for granted in 1226.

In the second place, the papacy has emerged supreme. The vicar of Christ is acknowledged to be the titular head of Christendom in spirituals and, to a limited degree, in temporals. Francis added tremendous weight to the prestige of the Roman see.

Lastly, the church is coming to control the state. The tendency, in theory and fact, during the early thirteenth century was for lay rulers to hand over spiritual responsibilities to the clergy, par excellence the pope. Kings and princes, although still considered in learned and in popular opinion to be wielders of sacred offices, are obliged to abandon some traditional constraints on the church, thus weakening their hold over their subjects. As the "arm" of the church body, the state's function, according to clerical writers, was to do the inferior work of protecting clerics and their lands, and punishing criminals.

In 1226 most Europeans believed in the desirability of a united Christendom. On the one hand, those of a Gregorian tendency stressed the order which should be imposed by the clergy and the papacy; prophecy should work closely with and at the bidding of the forces of order. On the other hand, those who stressed the necessity of prophetic witness, such as the Spiritualist Franciscans and the Cistercians, would have the "perfect"

Christians physically cut off from secular and ecclesiastical politics. But a third solution was possible: a federation of "national" states politically independent of Rome. Why not establish an equilibrium between church and state by restricting the church to spiritual affairs, and the individual secular states to temporal affairs—the Holy Roman Empire being only one among many states? At the time this solution was not foreseen because it was impossible for people to conceive of political powers in such terms. Feudal principalities and towns were as yet institutionally too rudimentary.

Our heart has ever burned with the desire to restore the ancient dignity of Rome and of Caesar, the Founder of the Roman Empire.

Frederick II

IV

FREDERICK THE GREAT AND ST LOUIS

FREDERICK II, THE GREAT (1194-1250)

Frederick II was the last universal Holy Roman Emperor. With him passed all hope of a revived empire or a united German monarchy. But Frederick was also an accomplice in the undoing of the *papal* monarchy. Frederick's desperate war with the papacy almost destroyed the pope's claim to head universal Christendom. After Innocent III had upset the delicate papal-imperial power balance in favor of St Peter, succeeding

121

popes took the next logical step: the attempt to eradi-
cate all imperial power in Italy. Since Frederick II was
committed to the conquest of Italy, no compromise was
possible. But the papacy's victory was pyrrhic. Christ's
seamless garment, His church on earth, was thereby rent
forever.

THE BOY FROM SICILY (1194-1208)

Since Frederick was the son of Emperor Henry VI (d.
1197) he was rightful heir to the throne. But the infant
Frederick's claims were ignored in Germany and Rome.
After Henry VI's brother, Philip, got himself elected
King of the Romans by the Hohenstaufen princes, Pope
Innocent III came out for the rival candidate, Otto, who
had to promise to relinquish imperial claims in Italy.
Hence he pressured Constance, the Sicilian wife of
Henry VI, to hand Sicily over to papal protection. Con-
stance agreed to let the pope control the Sicilian church
and to prevent the boy Frederick from ever becoming
Holy Roman Emperor. Innocent feared that Germany
and Sicily would suffocate the Papal States in a Hohenstaufen squeeze play.

The unfortunate child became a pawn in the bloody
power struggles involving Constance, her anti-German
supporters, Sicilian nobles (of divided loyalties), German adventurers who invaded Sicily, and papal armies.
Hustled from place to place Frederick was successively a
hostage of Sicilian factions, Germans, and papal legates.
This rough handling left emotional scars on the prized
heir of Sicily. In place of a real father, Frederick had
numerous tutors who offered him conflicting advice
concerning his future political role. As a result of this
unusual education the boy grew up distrustful of all
men. Forced to rely on his own inner resources, he preferred to wander alone in the magnificent garden near
the royal palace in Palermo. Throughout his life he re-

tained an almost pathological need for personal power and independence.

To escape mentally from the tumult of the civil wars raging throughout Sicily Frederick threw himself into his studies. This precocious wonderchild displayed remarkable skill in handling mathematical and philosophical problems. Before becoming an adult he spoke six languages including Arabic. He especially liked to read about his predecessors, the great Roman emperors and the Norman conquerors of Sicily. He dreamed of becoming another Caesar Augustus. In the rich, cosmopolitan culture of Sicily—a fusion of Norman, Roman, Byzantine, Lombard, Muslim—Frederick enlarged his intellectual awareness.

KING OF SICILY (1208-1212)

In 1208 Pope Innocent III permitted Frederick, now fourteen, to become king of Sicily. In the same year, Philip of Hohenstaufen was murdered, a welcome relief to the beleaguered Innocent. After arranging Frederick's marriage to Constance of Aragon, the pope got both Frederick and Otto, now undisputed emperor, to swear not to molest papal lands. But Otto broke his promise and invaded central and southern Italy. In retaliation the pope excommunicated Otto and conspired, with the help of Philip Augustus of France, to stir up revolts against Otto in Germany. Many German princes were only too glad to seize upon this excuse to repudiate the disliked Otto. In 1211 some German princes journeyed to Sicily and asked Frederick to become their king.

His wife and his councillors begged Frederick not to accept the German crown. How could Frederick abandon his kingdom which was now so sorely in need of a strong hand? He knew nothing of Germany and could not even speak the German language. Perhaps this strange lad believed that he could become a real monarch instead of the shadow king he was in Sicily. The title of King of the Romans* was magic to him. Was he not the true emperor, the son of Henry VI? After having been repeatedly ignored and humiliated by the pope, his own Hohenstaufen, and the Welfs (Otto), Frederick would get his revenge. In March 1212 Frederick set sail for Germany.

FREDERICK IN GERMANY (1212-1220)

Before Innocent III would give his blessing to Frederick's elevation he forced him to recognize papal claims in Sicily and the Papal States. Frederick agreed that his newborn son, Henry, would become king of Sicily. Innocent III feared that Frederick might try to retain Sicily while he was Holy Roman Emperor. But the treason of Otto left the pope no other choice.

Once in Germany Frederick quickly got lay princes, bishops, and townsmen to abandon Otto. The young king promised money, lands, and concessions to all who would recognize his authority. To his dismay Frederick realized that he was becoming dependent upon the princes who had invited him to their land. They did not want a strong king but a figurehead who would protect their interests. With their help Frederick by 1215 had overcome most of Otto's supporters. Innocent III persuaded the Lateran Council to accept Frederick as King of the Romans. In just three years Frederick had secured his position in Germany.

But after 1215 Frederick became restless. He was painfully aware of his lack of actual power. The boy from Sicily found that the civil wars of 1198-1212 and the princely privileges he parceled out from 1212 to 1215 left him with little more than nominal influence

*When the German princes elected their candidate, he received the title King of the Romans. It was presumed that this German king would then be crowned *Emperor* of the Romans by the pope in Rome. Emperors usually used their imperial title to lay claim to Italy as part of the so-called Holy Roman Empire.

within the great principalities. The romance and glory of his triumphant march throughout Germany in 1212 were gone. He was frustrated in his humble role as peacemaker in a war-trodden yet volatile realm. He was weary of listening to the petty complaints of churchmen, townsmen, and nobles, who cared only for their local concerns. Frederick had no emotional attachment to this accursed country with its icy winters, damp castles, and boorish people. His body was in Germany, but his soul in Sicily.

After 1215 Frederick sought a way to get out of Germany and back to Sicily—without forfeiting his German title and his alliances with German princes. But how could any pope allow a Hohenstaufen to keep both Germany and Sicily? Unexpectedly, the opportunity came when the pope's crusade in Egypt got bogged down in 1219. After ignoring Frederick's offers for two years to lead a crusade to the Holy Land, Pope Honorius III (1217-27) was forced to turn to Frederick for assistance. Frederick replied that he was only too willing to take the cross, but on condition that the pope crown him emperor in Rome. Frederick did not tell the pope that he was arranging for the election of his son Henry as German king. Frederick's plan was to get Henry elected German king, take the Holy Land from the Muslims, and then return to his beloved Sicily once the emperor had rescued the papal crusade. Frederick's seemingly impossible goals hinged on the success of his crusade.

To get the German prince-bishops to agree to the election of his son Henry, Frederick in 1219 gave them such enormous concessions that they emerged as virtually independent princes within the empire. Any hope of reestablishing a centralized German monarchy was abandoned as a result of this historic act. Although **many bi**shops had been usurping royal rights since 1198, these usurpations were now made legal and general.

With the support of most bishops Henry was elected
German king the following year.

Accordingly, Pope Honorius III in 1220 crowned
Frederick emperor in Rome and even allowed Frederick
to retain the title King of Sicily for his lifetime. Frederick then returned to Sicily to make preparations for the
crusade to Jerusalem. In 1211 Frederick had been a
helpless papal ward caught in the cross fire of the Sicilian wars; now, nine years later, Frederick returned as
Holy Roman Emperor. Frederick called this reversal of
fortune a "divine miracle."

SICILY (1220-1225)

Frederick discovered that royal authority in Sicily
had passed into the hands of princes, prelates, and
townsmen. The chaos of 1198-1220 had enfeebled the
crown's sovereignty. Frederick's first act was to issue
decrees at Capua which ordered that all privileges in the
realm were to be examined personally by the emperor.
If the emperor deemed a privilege to be held illegally, it
was thereby declared void. Thus began Frederick's war
on the barons. He played one group off against another
in his attempt to recover the castles, revenues, and lands
of the crown.

As it turned out Frederick's pause in Sicily became
indefinitely extended. Each time the pope demanded
that he fulfill his crusade pledge, Frederick put him off
with a different excuse. While Frederick was attacking
rebellious Muslims in western Sicily, he notified the
pope that he had a Christian duty to suppress infidels at
home before he could engage them in Jerusalem. To
settle the Muslim problem Frederick exported his Muslim captives to Lucera in southern Italy. Here they were
permitted to worship Allah; later these same Muslims
comprised loyal regiments in Frederick's wars in northern Italy! The Roman Curia was scandalized to learn of

this importation of God's enemies just a few miles from the Papal States.

Frederick felt he could not leave Sicily while his reconquest was as yet incomplete. He revived the royal prerogatives and the judicial system. No one in the kingdom could bear arms without the emperor's consent. Frederick appointed high officials in the cities. Most commercial activities, especially in the port towns, were regulated by the royal court. To protect his trade monopolies Frederick built a formidable navy and merchant marine. An elaborate tax system brought in a steady flow of revenue. A tough criminal code included the punishment of blasphemy. Jews and prostitutes were to wear distinguishing dress. In violation of former agreements with the Curia Frederick moved to control ecclesiastical elections.

By 1225 Sicily was on the way to becoming the most centralized kingdom in Christendom. Frederick had neutralized the barons and created a powerful state which combined the methods of an absolute despot with those of a feudal suzerain. For the purpose of filling his expanding bureaucracy with trained jurists and notaries he founded a university at Naples.

Pope Honorius and the Curia watched this power-buildup with horror. When Queen Constance died in 1222 Honorius arranged for Frederick to marry Isabella, heiress to the kingdom of Jerusalem. If the Holy Spirit could not move Frederick to sail to the Holy Land, perhaps his lust for power would induce him to lay claim to his overseas territory. When Frederick again postponed his departure Honorius issued an ultimatum in 1225: Frederick would be excommunicated if he failed to set out on crusade by 15 August 1227.

LOMBARDY (1226)

The supremely confident Frederick summoned a diet at Cremona for Easter 1226. Ostensibly the diet was to

recruit men and money for the crusade, and consider
ways to exterminate heresy in Lombardy. But the Lombards saw the diet as a declaration of war on their independence. Visions of Frederick Barbarossa's invading
army danced in Lombard heads. The Curia saw in the
diet the first sign of a renewed Hohenstaufen presence
in Romana, Spoleto, and Ancona. Immediately some
Lombard cities formed an offensive and defensive alliance, and blocked the Alpine passes to prevent King
Henry and the German princes from attending the diet
of Cremona—which never took place.

Frederick's attempt at a show of strength in northern
Italy made the Lombards willing to ally with the
papacy. Frederick, the ruler of a powerful state, had
little to fear from the Lombard towns and the Papal
States. But the emperor's ill-considered march into
Lombardy gave the pope a pretext for enlisting the help
of Lombards in his war on Frederick.

THE STRANGE CRUSADE (1227-1229)

After massive preparations Frederick with an army of
40,000 finally embarked at Brindisi for the crusade in
August 1227. But Frederick caught the plague and was
forced to return to Brindisi where hundreds had already
perished from the disease. He sent an embassy to the
newly elected pope, Gregory IX, to explain the delay.
But Gregory was in no mood to bargain and refused
even to receive the imperial delegation. On 29 September 1229 Gregory excommunicated the emperor.

Pope Gregory IX (1227-1241), formerly Cardinal
Ugolino,* was different from his predecessor. Whereas
the aged Honorius III was easygoing and flexible,
Gregory IX committed the papacy to a full attack on
Frederick's pretensions in Lombardy, the Papal States,
and Sicily. The pope would lift the ban only if Freder-

*See above, pp. 108-113.

ick returned Sicily to papal overlordship. In his encyclical letters Gregory blamed Frederick for the failure of the crusade. He even accused Frederick of deliberately choosing Brindisi as the embarkation port in order to kill off the crusaders.

To vindicate himself before the rulers of Europe and to retain his diplomatic leverage Frederick, hard pressed for money, set sail for the Holy Land with a tiny army. During Frederick's absence Gregory IX sent into Sicily an army commanded by the father of Frederick's late wife, Isabella of Jerusalem! Europe was shocked to witness this invasion of the lands of a crusader (forbidden by canon law), even though excommunicated. When Gregory tried to stir up a revolt in Germany the princes lined up behind Frederick. Indeed, the German prelates refused to publish the papal ban of excommunication in their churches. Frederick's favors to the princes had served him well.

Frederick recovered Jerusalem and Bethlehem without lifting a sword. He made a ten-year truce with his friend al-Kamil, Sultan of Egypt. The Curia belittled this deal struck with the infidel. The Muslims, for their part, did not know what to make of this Arabic-speaking crusader who was given to making snide remarks about the Christian faith. It was hard to trust a man who broke all the rules. Nevertheless, Frederick had achieved by diplomacy what could not be achieved by force. When he returned to Sicily the papal armies crumbled. Forced to yield, Gregory IX received Frederick back into the Catholic fold. Most cardinals insisted that Gregory try to maintain the traditional imperial-papal coexistence for the sake of peace.

FREDERICK'S MODEL KINGDOM: SICILY (1230-1250)

The kingdom of Sicily was the marvel of Christendom. Rulers throughout Europe envied Frederick's solid position as the head of an efficient bureaucracy centralized at the royal court. Frederick's judicial and fiscal hold on Sicily continued to tighten after his return in 1230. His system of laws was the most uniform of any principality at the time.

Frederick invited scholars and artists to visit and settle at his court. Himself a poet he encouraged the writing of poetry in Latin and the vernacular. The royal court became renowned for its scholarly achievements in astronomy, medicine, translations, history, mathematics. Frederick spent many evenings exchanging ideas with some of the most brilliant philosophers and scientists of the day. His broad interests extended to Arabic and Jewish philosophy, much to the scandal of pious cardinals in Rome. He wrote a long treatise *On the Art of Hunting with Birds*, still recognized as one of the finest scientific studies on falconry. In this book Frederick assured his readers that his conclusions were based on personal experience with falcons. Venerable authorities, including Aristotle, had to be rejected if their opinions did not conform to empirical observation. The truly rational mind could not be bound by tradition.

As a patron of art Frederick was particularly interested in music, sculpture, and architecture. His hunting castles reveal a taste for northern European, Arabic, Byzantine, and Sicilian styles. He created a new synthesis of several cultural traditions. It was fitting that a Roman Caesar, as he referred to himself, have a public art which expressed his political ideal.

TROUBLE IN GERMANY (1230-1237)

Frederick's son, Henry, grew up in Germany. Unfortunately for his father, Henry took his role as German king seriously and attempted to reassert the royal authority. Henry allied with the wealthy towns and lesser nobles against the great princes. But following the princes' military triumph over Henry, Frederick reluctantly made far-reaching concessions to the lay princes who became virtually independent in their principalities. With the emperor's privileges to the bishop-princes in 1220 and the lay princes in 1231, the Holy Roman Emperor's power in Germany was becoming little more than an empty title.

Frederick expected Henry to cater to the princes and help him in his Italian wars. Frederick needed troops, revenue, and the support of the princes to ward off papal aggressions in Lombardy and Germany. Germany was the center piece of the empire. Moreover, Frederick needed the imperial title as his legal claim to central and northern Italy. But Henry rebelled again and even formed an alliance with Milan. This time the enraged Frederick sentenced his son to life imprisonment. Fearing execution, Henry later committed suicide by riding his horse over a cliff. In 1237 Frederick got the princes to elect his other son Conrad (by Isabella of Jerusalem) as king in Germany.

ALL OUT WAR:
FREDERICK vs. GREGORY IX
(1235-1241)

When Frederick invaded Lombardy in 1235 Pope Gregory IX launched his attack on the emperor. The pope sent legates and friars into Lombardy, Germany, and Sicily to drum up support for the papal side. After Frederick's impressive military victory over Milanese forces in 1237, the pope asked the German princes to elect a new king. Gregory IX then preached a "crusade" against Frederick, and appealed to France and England for help. Failing to elicit a response from outside Italy, he excommunicated Frederick in 1239. But to no avail. The overused papal excommunication was losing its sting. Frederick's soldiers subdued most of the Papal States and were closing in on Rome. In a desperate eleventh-hour gamble Gregory IX led a procession

through the streets of Rome carrying the bones of
Saints Peter and Paul. The Roman people would burn in
hell, Gregory thundered, if they did not protect the
holy relics. Suddenly the Roman mob, which jeered
Gregory only moments before, made the sign of the
cross and swore to defend the church. Upon learning of
this turnabout by the fickle populace Frederick outside
the gates of Rome disbanded his army and returned to
Sicily.

But the unpopular Gregory was still relatively isolated. Many cardinals and Roman citizens pressured the
pope to come to terms with the emperor, who skillfully
exploited antipapal grievances in Rome and throughout
Italy. While Frederick never had large armies he was able
to side with factions within the cities and to join any
northern city which feared the economic and military
might of Milan. The more disunity in Italy, the more
leverage Frederick had over the pope. Only the fierce
independent spirit of the great families and the commercial rivalries among large communes permitted the
emperor to be a factor in Italian politics. Moreover, a
few Italians believed that a strong imperial presence
would help maintain the status quo and bring peace to a
troubled Italy.

Frederick enhanced his diplomatic oneupmanship by
playing the game of Roman Caesarism. He traveled with
a magnificent entourage which included a menagerie of
elephants, pandas, giraffes, cheetahs, and of course falcons. His harem of Arab dancing girls was always welcome. The Italians, acutely conscious of their Roman
past, appreciated every gesture of "their" emperor. People who were disaffected with the clerical church found
an emotional outlet in the ceremonies and symbols of
Caesar. Above all, the mounting criticism of the
church's wealth and political power worked to Frederick's advantage. Frederick preached that *he*, not the
worldly pope, was protecting the church and the true
faith. Only the Roman emperor, read the imperial

rhetoric, could restore the Catholic church to the purity of the primitive church. It was rumored that Frederick was the new Messiah.

For Gregory IX Frederick was the Antichrist who would bring ruin to God's church. Hence any means was justified in ridding the world of this diabolical pestilence. Gregory was persuaded that Frederick planned to seize the Papal States and Rome itself, and then appoint his own pope. The bride of Christ would then be controlled by Satan and all his works.

When word got out that Frederick was preparing to summon an ecumenical council which was to depose him, Gregory IX quickly called his own council. Naturally he invited those prelates who were hostile to Frederick. Realizing he had been out-flanked, Frederick warned all European powers that any prelate on his way to the pope's general council would be arrested. This reckless threat reveals how badly Frederick's confidence had been shaken by his repeated defeats in Lombardy. After 1239 Frederick's methods were getting as extreme as his enemy's. Gregory IX ignored Frederick's warning and encouraged the prelates to journey by sea to Rome. The more daring of the prelates set sail from Genoa on 28 April 1241 in 60 ships. Hiding in the Tuscan Archipelago Frederick's fleet pounced on the Genoese navy and nearly annihilated it. Three Genoese galleys went down with all hands. Among the 4,000 prisoners taken were 100 church dignitaries, including two cardinals. Only three Genoese ships escaped. Frederick's distinguished captives spent the rest of their days in Sicilian dungeons.

Frederick prevented the general council but damaged his image. Henceforth it was difficult for a prince, lay or ecclesiastical, to defend publicly Frederick's feud with the pope. No longer could Frederick feign the oppressed martyr who was valiantly trying to rid the church of a bad pope. Soon after this sacrilegious assault on the church Frederick laid another (unsuccessful) siege on

Rome. The unyielding Pope Gregory IX died on 21
August 1241.

About this time Frederick's prestige was further
weakened by his failure to go to Germany in a time of
crisis. Since 1239 fierce hordes of tribesmen from Asia
had swept across Russia and Poland and were entering
Germany. Frederick wrote circular letters promising his
return to Germany to lead a defensive war against the
Mongols. But he was engaged in his Italian campaigns
and many Germans never forgave him for abandoning
them. The Mongols eventually returned to Asia to settle
a dynastic dispute.

THE CHURCH WITHOUT A HEAD
(1241-1243)

Only nine cardinals were left in Rome to elect a new
pope. The Senator of Rome, an enemy of Frederick,
arrested the cardinals and threw them into a dilapidated
palace. The open roof in this prison exposed them to
rain and the excrement from the guards who, stationed
on the roof, used the open room as a latrine. Several of
the cardinals would die from this abuse. But despite the
pressure from the senator the prisoners were deadlocked
between two candidates, one desirous of peace with the
emperor, the other an ardent foe of the Hohenstaufen.
They finally elected a compromise candidate who soon
died. After two years of intrigues and pressures from
Frederick and princes throughout Europe, the cardinals
elected one of their own, a canon lawyer who took the
name Innocent IV.

COUNCIL OF LYON (1245)

At the insistence of the king of France and the
Roman Curia the new pope reopened negotiations with
Frederick whose recent military reversals made him
amenable to peace. Before Pope Innocent IV

(1243-1254) would absolve the emperor all church lands were to be returned to the papacy. A personal interview between pope and emperor was arranged. But on his way to the meeting Innocent IV slipped out of Rome and, disguised as a soldier, sailed to his hometown of Genoa. From here Innocent sent letters to European princes asking them to receive him. But all refused. They were aware that Innocent's scheme was to summon a general council which would depose Frederick. Fearing an imperial attack on Rome and wary of the fickle Roman mob, Innocent felt he had to hold the council a safe distance from Italy. The pope was finally allowed to settle at Lyon, technically a part of the empire but in fact independent. Innocent had won the first round. He made it appear that he was driven from the holy city by a revengeful and brutal emperor.

To prepare for the coming council Innocent IV dispensed benefices and other concessions to French prelates who flocked to Lyon seeking papal favors. Innocent's invitation list for the council did not include Frederick although the pope did summon the emperor in a sermon. Frederick's military position in northern and central Italy was deteriorating; Sicilians were resisting the heavy imperial taxes. To ensure the succession of his son Conrad, Frederick, to the surprise of all, offered to accept the papal demands and would even spend the remainder of his life in the Holy Land! But the pope declined the offer.

The "general" council contained prelates mainly from France, Spain, England, three countries still angry with Frederick for his assault on their colleagues at the last would-be council; a few prelates from Lombardy also appeared. Innocent IV opened the council on 26 June 1245 with a litany of charges against the emperor. He accused Frederick of disobeying the church, despoiling church lands, breaking his oath, committing sacrilege, and allying with Muslims. Frederick was a heretic, a lecher who kept Muslim harems, a cruel tyrant who kept

his wife in the charge of eunuchs. The pope implied that
Frederick was responsible for the successes of the Mon-
gols in Russia and Germany, and of the Khwarismians in
Jerusalem.

Frederick's representative, Thaddeus, replied to these
charges before the assembly. Everyone at the council
knew that these charges and rebuttals were smoke
screens to hide the pope's real grievance: Frederick's
political ambitions in Lombardy and the Papal States.
Realizing that the council was rigged against the emperor, Thaddeus begged Frederick to put in a personal
appearance. There was an outside chance that Frederick's presence might forestall his excommunication. But
Frederick refused to go. Wallowing in self pity, he
would not grovel before his archenemy. Besides, if the
council declared him deposed, his diplomatic arsenal
would be spent. Frederick preferred to challenge the
legitimacy of the council on the grounds that it was not
ecumenical. Frederick neglected to point out that he
himself prevented the German and Sicilian prelates from
attending.

Fearing the appearance of Frederick and his army
Innocent IV speeded up the proceedings. On 17 July
1245 Frederick II was excommunicated and deposed.
All subjects of Sicily and the empire were released from
their oaths of allegiance to Frederick. Interestingly,
Lombardy was not mentioned in the formal sentence of
the council.

Frederick responded to this deposition by writing letters to the princes and clergy of Europe. He accused
Innocent of acting out of personal enmity. Frederick
warned the princes that if the pope were permitted to
depose the emperor, no crown would be secure. Princes
should band together to resist the political pretentions
of the Roman church. The pope should abandon his
material possessions and live like the poor Christ. By
identifying his cause with the popular criticism of the
clergy Frederick was hitting the pope in his weak spot.

While many princes privately applauded Frederick's attack on the Curia, it was politically impossible for them to declare open war on their own bishops and abbots. Princes had to deal discreetly with powerful prelates whose support was a political necessity. While Frederick's rhetorical blasts against clerical worldliness found sympathetic listeners, it brought him little diplomatic or military help.

POPE INNOCENT IV'S "CRUSADE" AGAINST FREDERICK

Innocent IV's war on Frederick was total. The pope sent friars into Germany to preach a "crusade" against the Antichrist. A "crusader" was promised a papal indulgence; if he chose not to fight he could receive the same indulgence in return for a money payment. By means of extensive bribes Innocent set up his own German king, Henry Raspe, who died a year later. From Lyon the pope conspired with factions in towns throughout Italy to encourage rebellions against the emperor. To pay for this expensive war Innocent IV levied extraordinary taxes, and exchanged benefices and privileges for money. It might be noted that prelates exploited the pope's preoccupation with the emperor by getting special favors in return for their financial and diplomatic support. The prelates knew all along that only the pope could survive the war.

Papal agents throughout Europe reported the most hair-raising atrocities allegedly committed by Frederick. They also encouraged the strange rumors already widespread about the famous *Stupor Mundi*, (The Wonder of the World) as Frederick was commonly known. It was said that Frederick once placed a condemned criminal in a barrel and ordered his courtiers to watch the barrel until the man died. Since no one saw a soul leave the barrel Frederick concluded that the soul died with the body. It was said that he disemboweled a living man immediately after the person ate dinner in order to examine the process of digestion. It was said that he had some children brought up in complete silence to determine which language the children would speak "naturally." Alas, the children spoke no language and died from lack of affection. It was rumored that Frederick once said that the world had been deceived by three great imposters: Moses, Mohammed, and Jesus Christ. Papal agents helped to spread similar gossip about Frederick's unorthodox opinions and weird scientific (diabolical it was said) experiments. How many of these tales are true will never be known.

Many Europeans found Innocent IV's methods repulsive. The pope was using his authority as Christ's vicar to carry on his personal feud with Frederick for control of Italy. While the pope was launching a "crusade" against Frederick in Germany, King Louis of France was preparing a crusade against the infidel in Jerusalem which had fallen in 1244. It seemed as if the pontiff, the traditional organizer of the holy war, were blocking the real crusade against Christ's foes in the East. Granted the crusade was hardly popular in Europe at this time, it was still disconcerting to know that the Holy Father was taking from Germany Frisian soldiers (who were already promised to King Louis by Innocent) and paying them to rebel against Frederick—who in any case was not considered a heretic by most Germans.

FREDERICK II'S TRAGIC END
(1245-1250)

After his excommunication Frederick lost all sense of balance. Frantically he attempted to keep the loyalty of his Italian allies, who were losing faith in the imperial protective umbrella. The emperor suffered military and diplomatic reversals in central and northern Italy. Instead of suing for peace Frederick attempted to wage war on a hundred fronts at once. He trusted no one and saw conspiracies everywhere. Frederick accused his long-time friend and advisor, Piero della Vigna, of plotting against his life. (It was widely believed that Innocent IV instigated this plot.) When Frederick's own doctor tried to poison him, he had the doctor blinded and tortured to death. Frederick died in 1250 still trying to reassert his imperial authority.

Frederick never understood that his delusions of becoming another Roman Caesar had no chance of success. His ferocious drive for power obscured political reality. The imperial presence in the Papal States and Lombardy could be maintained only because rival communes and lords wanted to use Frederick's support in their own petty feuds. The imperial mercenary armies were ill-equipped to take on the aroused Lombard towns. When particular towns found Frederick's presence inconvenient, they simply ignored him or joined his enemies. Moreover, Frederick's makeshift bureaucracy outside Sicily was no match for the entrenched legatine and judicial system of the papacy. In a prolonged struggle between pope and emperor the superior material and spiritual weapons of St Peter would triumph.

At first, Frederick II wanted to unite Germany and Sicily. After 1230 his pretensions in the rest of Italy increased with each diplomatic success. If Frederick had chosen to remain in Sicily he would have been remembered as one of the greatest rulers Sicily ever had. As it happened, Frederick left Germany and Sicily in shambles. By committing his imperial resources to Italy, Frederick virtually completed the process in Germany started during the Investiture Controversy of the eleventh century: the aggrandizement of a few territorial princes. By committing his Sicilian resources to the rest of Italy, Frederick lost Sicily for the Hohenstaufen. Sicily became an international pawn in the late thirteenth century.

SIGNIFICANCE OF THE
IMPERIAL-PAPAL CONFLICT

Any possibility of making the Holy Roman Empire the focal point of European unity perished with Frederick the Great in 1250. The struggle between Frederick and the popes left both Germany and Italy ever more divided. As a result, Germany and Italy were too fragmented for either to assume the role of international peacekeeper or superpower.

But the papacy also suffered irreparable damage. The moral supremacy of the papal monarchy was a casualty in the wars led by Popes Gregory IX and Innocent IV. While he lived, Pope Innocent III had been considered a disinterested arbiter genuinely devoted to the reform of the whole church, though a few might have grumbled about his methods. As the head of Christendom he had usually treated all sides fairly. Innocent IV, on the other hand, was a *partisan* who mustered the institutional and spiritual instruments of the Fisherman to topple a political foe. Whereas Innocent III had subordinated his interference in Germany to his plans for universal church reform and the crusade, Innocent IV subordinated reform and the crusade to his attack on Frederick. Whereas Innocent III had been internationalist in outlook, Innocent IV's eyes were riveted to Italy. Europeans criticized Innocent IV for using his sacred office for political advantage. Following Frederick's death Innocent IV called in foreign troops to invade Sicily and destroy the remaining Hohenstaufen.

Pope Gregory VII would probably not have recognized his ideal in the papacy of Innocent IV. To be sure Gregory VII wanted the clerical church to function independently as a centralized unit apart from lay society. But as the papacy from 1085 to 1250 struggled for independence, it became even more enmeshed in the political life of Italy. Frederickan propaganda notwithstanding, Innocent IV was not an evil person. He was

simply trying to free the papacy from imperial interference so that it could perform its proper task of leading Christians to heaven. No responsible pope or prelate
could allow the church to be manipulated by laymen for
selfish ends. Besides, prelates were acknowledged to
have legitimate temporal commitments. But by 1250
the curial bureaucracy had become so sophisticated and
so powerful that any move to remove a troublesome
emperor from Italy involved extensive intervention in
Italian ecclesiastical and secular politics. Non-Italians
too often interpreted Innocent IV's request for tax
money as papal lust for political power in Italy. In the
twelfth century the papal monarchy had been enthusiastically welcomed for its ability to settle disputes in the
interests of all. By the mid-thirteenth century, however,
papal institutions were forcing the Curia deeper into the
mud of Italian politics. Papal institutions were taking on
a life of their own. By attempting to preserve the existing curial structure, cardinals tended to forget why the
church organization was created in the first place. Popes
were becoming victims of the papacy; the means was
becoming an end in itself. The Hohenstaufen presence in
Italy forced the papal monarchy to become rigid and
sometimes unresponsive to the spiritual needs of all
Christians. Innocent III had had St Francis at the controls of his machine; Innocent IV had only the machine.

The imperial-papal struggle exhausted and degraded
both sides. What was needed was another "emperor"
who was both saint and soldier. The prophet on horse-
back would come from France.

KING LOUIS IX OF FRANCE (1226-1270)

After hearing mass, the king often went to the wood of
Vincennes, where he would sit with his back against an oak.
Those who had any lawsuit could come to speak to him. If
he saw anything needing correction he would himself intervene to make the adjustment.

Joinville

The power vacuum left in the aftermath of the imperial-papal conflicts was filled by a French monarch, Louis IX (1214-1270, canonized a saint in 1297). But St Louis made no attempt to replace the universalism of Pope Innocent IV or Frederick II with his own brand of universalism. Instead, he sought to construct a particularist state, the kingdom of France. This state, a prototype of the later nation state, would serve to dismantle the Gregorian church. Ironically it was the papacy which created conditions favorable to the growth of the French national state. Indeed, nationalism and the nation might never have been realized without the drive by the holy see to forge a centralized church.

ST LOUIS' MINORITY (1226-1234)

King Louis VIII (1223-1226) died while on campaign against the Cathars in southern France. Immediately the barons conspired to revolt against his widow, Blanche of Castille, regent for her teenage son. The barons, alarmed at the growing power of the monarchy under Philip Augustus and Louis VIII, sought to regain something of their ancient privileges. As an excuse for rebellion the nobles complained of Blanche's foreign origins, her sex, and her alleged contempt of the peerage. They took heart at the success of their counterparts in England who forced their king to sign the Magna Carta.

But Blanche turned out to be a formidable foe. Without hesitation she raised a large army and marched from Paris to the southwest. Fortunately for Blanche Count Theobald of Champagne withdrew from the conspiracy and declared for the king. Though he had never met the queen, the 27-year-old Theobald composed love poems for Blanche, a widow of 40. Blanche must have been amused and pleased by these overtures. Henceforth her main enemies were Count Peter of Brittany and King Henry III of England who exploited baronial discontent in an attempt to regain his continental fiefs. Against conventional rules of warfare Blanche took the war to Count Peter's own home and stormed his castle in the dead of winter (1229), forcing him to capitulate. Blanche's whirlwind campaign in the south, west, and east finally crushed the rebellion. Henry III retreated to England. The rising failed because the magnates, having no tradition of concerted action, could not unite. They were as suspicious of each other as they were of the royal family.

The revolt impressed on the young king, who accompanied his mother on these campaigns, the need to prevent such feudal disorder in the future. Many nobles and townsmen were grateful for the monarchy's suppression of the anarchy. When in 1234 Blanche had her son married to Marguerite of Provence—the beginning of royal inroads into the southeast—Louis IX attained his majority. This extraordinary woman would continue to rule with her son until her death in 1252.

THE FEUDAL WARRIOR (1234-1248)

St Louis saw himself as a Christian king who was called to do battle in defense of his rights. In 1242 he broke up a coalition of rebel barons and knights in Poitou. Henceforth Louis was never to face a serious uprising. He strengthened royal control within his domain and even expanded the domain in the South.

Blanche raised her offspring in the spirit of her strict Spanish Catholicism. She once remarked that she would rather see her son die than have him commit a mortal sin. Louis built the Cistercian monastery of Royaumont which was soon to become his favorite refuge. During these visits to Royaumont he would dress like a monk and follow the daily routine of the monks. This form of religious sentiment—the vicarious experience of the monastic life—was not uncommon among conservative nobles. Just as conventional was the king's yearning for relics. At enormous cost to his people Louis purchased the Crown of Thorns, and built a chapel in Paris to house it. His Sainte Chapelle remains one of the masterpieces of gothic art.

In 1244 St Louis fell ill and swore that if he recovered he would lead a crusade to the Holy Land. Recover he did, and despite the pleas of his mother, wife, and advisors, Louis could not be swayed to forgo his crusading vow. Immediately he began preparations for the venture.

When Pope Innocent IV called his council in Lyon St Louis pressured him to make the council levy a tax on the French clergy for the royal crusade. Repeatedly St Louis attempted to mediate the dispute between Frederick II and Innocent IV, but the pope refused to negotiate with the Hohenstaufen. Louis complained that the pope was taxing the French clergy for the "crusade" against the emperor, thereby depriving him of revenues for the real crusade in the East. The king had to placate both pope and emperor, for he needed their support if his crusade were to succeed.

To complicate matters for the king, the barons of France in 1246 formed a military league against the prelates whose temporal power was encroaching on lay jurisdictions. St Louis took the barons' protest to the pope who ignored the royal request and excommunicated the barons for usurping church liberties. It should be added that the French bishops were at the same time complaining to the pope about the attacks of St Louis upon *their* temporal rights!

Although he did not realize it at the time, St Louis' departure for the crusade was politically efficacious. By being absent he avoided having to choose sides in the internal disputes. In the midst of domestic unrest and the threat of an English invasion St Louis felt it was more important to regain Jerusalem for Christ. But before he left he sent out *enquêteurs* to investigate the activities of all royal officials. France was astounded to witness their king summon his own agents to account.

As a crusader St Louis wanted to settle temporal affairs and right any wrongs since he might well never return from the East. But the *enquêteur* system had far-reaching political results for the monarchy; these roving inquisitors (reminiscent of the days of Charlemagne) convinced many that Louis was on the side of justice.

During the stormy period 1226-1248 St Louis acted as if he were a traditional feudal suzerain safeguarding regional custom. Despite his confrontations, with the French clergy and the barons, he always claimed that he was defending the rights of his domain as well as the rights of his vassals. His stern but never vindictive treatment of his enemies earned him respect. After appointing his mother regent St Louis set sail in 1248.

CRUSADE (1248-1254)

St Louis planned to conquer Egypt before taking the holy places. The crusaders took Damietta but afterwards were checked on the way to Cairo. The retreating king and many of his nobles were captured and held for ransom by the Muslims. Arab doctors cured St Louis' dysentery. After long negotiations the sultan agreed to release Louis and his barons in exchange for Damietta and 800,000 bezants. While many of the nobles headed for home the undaunted Louis went on to Acre.

St Louis soon realized how hopeless was the task of recovering the Holy Land. He waited for an outbreak of civil war among the sultans or possibly the conversion of the Mongols to Christianity. Getting additional help from Europe was difficult since crusades were no longer popular and even the pope was embarrassed by this king's crusading zeal. Back in Paris, poets were satirizing the king's adventure. When Blanche died in 1252 Louis still refused to give up. At last in 1254 broken in body and spirit the king returned to his realm.

ST LOUIS' IDEAL OF JUSTICE (1254-1270)

Upon his return St Louis set to work "reforming" his kingdom. For Louis, reform meant the enforcement of local custom. To this end St Louis organized regular circuits of his *enquêteurs*. More significantly the king turned the Parlement of Paris* into a permanent tribunal. Originally the Parlement was the name given to the King's Court when it sat as a judicial court. After 1254 the Parlement's primary functions were to hear appeals from lower courts, to try special cases in the first instance, and to review the rulings of lower courts. Gradually a concept of appellate jurisdiction was formed as the Parlement evolved into a final court of appeals. This tribunal's reputation for fairness was enhanced by its occasional rulings against the king himself. While St Louis allowed the Parlement to function independently, he carefully selected its members (both cleric and lay, the latter mainly from the petty nobility) and frequently sat in on its sessions.

St Louis' standards for his officials were high. In 1256 he drew up an ordinance for all royal officials. All had to swear in public that they would "do justice to all, without respect of persons, to the poor as well as to the rich" and would not take bribes. To set a good example officials were to refrain from dice and keep out of taverns, and not malign God and His saints. Baillis caught exceeding their jurisdiction would be punished by the king personally.

So self-righteous was St Louis in his pursuit of justice that he was incapable of seeing the contradictions in his policy. In the name of the high principle of justice his interference in local justice was often arbitrary; overzealous royal agents stretched the king's "rights" to the

*The Parlement of Paris was basically a judicial arm of the king. In England the Parliament had more diverse functions; it could even act as a brake on royal power.

limit. After 1254 St Louis acted increasingly as if he were a sovereign king, a supreme judge, and a maker of laws. He issued *établissements*, sort of executive decrees, which touched on questions of private morality and public law. He made blasphemy a crime. His Parlement sometimes altered local procedural law and set judicial precedents. "Bad customs" were abolished. He sometimes failed to distinguish between his domain and the entire kingdom. As the number of plaintiffs rushing to the Parlement increased, local feudal justice was effectively being eroded.

Many Frenchmen at the time attributed the relative peace and prosperity to St Louis' policies. Trade and agriculture flourished. Money flowed freely, assisted by the king's new coinage. In Europe France set the pace in education, philosophy, theology, literature, sculpture, architecture, stained glass. The French language was widely adopted outside the kingdom. Paris was the leading city of the West. St Louis developed a distinct court style of gothic art.

Professors of theology and philosophy, jurists, and administrators groped for a concept of kingship which included public sovereignty within the realm. They saw in the king the only hope of curbing feudal disorder and the worldly pretensions of the higher clergy, including the pope. They were intrigued with the idea of a rational political order which could function for the material and spiritual benefit of all (the "common good"), not just for the privileged few. They borrowed freely from feudal law, civil and canon law, natural law. To circumvent papal claims of supreme authority they needed a political theory which was not derived from the church. These attempts to justify and modernize St Louis' monarchy were the expressions of France's more urbanized and sophisticated members who wanted to diminish feudal holdovers from a more rural and primitive past.

Of these subtle theories St Louis understood little.
More old-fashioned, he convinced himself that his fre-
quent extortions of money from his subjects were
merely exercises of his "feudal" prerogatives and of his
rights as lord of his domain. After 1254 St Louis wore a
friar's habit and appointed Franciscans and Dominicans
to high offices. He appointed his close friend, the Franciscan Eudes, to the powerful see of Rouen. After 1254
Louis' religious outlook was more mendicant than
monastic. For him the king's chief duty was to Christianize society, a duty which also implied the furtherance
of material prosperity and temporal justice. The state
was not an evil necessitated by man's base nature; it was
natural and willed by the God of salvation.

St Louis was popular among his people because he
had a conservative image. Unlike his arrogant grandfather, Philip Augustus, St Louis seemed to behave as
people said a king should behave. One heard whispers
that Charlemagne had returned from the grave.

THE KING, THE FRENCH CLERGY,
THE PAPACY

St Louis had a deep reverence for the church and the
clergy. He followed the church's teaching and protected
the rights of clerics against lay lords and towns. But St
Louis clashed often with the higher clergy over issues
involving the church's *temporal* jurisdiction.

The struggle of Blanche and St Louis against the
bishop of Beauvais illustrates the royal approach. In
1232 when the rich citizens of Beauvais put up their
candidate for mayor, the poor selected a rival candidate.
To prevent bloodshed St Louis appointed his own
choice, Robert of Muret. The citizens showed their dis-
pleasure by rioting. In the scuffle Robert was beaten up
and expelled from the city. The bishop of Beauvais,
Milon, warned St Louis to keep out of the affair. But
Louis and Blanche entered the city, slapped hundreds of

rioters into prison, and laid a stiff fine on the city and
the bishop. When Milon objected, Louis seized his
property. Milon appealed to his superior, the archbishop
of Reims, who had a synod of bishops set up a commission to investigate the matter. But Louis refused to
recognize the commission's authority. The bishops
answered by laying an interdict on the entire archbishopric. Soon the chief prince-bishops were lined up
against the king since they feared that their submission
would establish a precedent for future royal aggressions
against the church. They appealed to Pope Gregory IX
who agreed with the bishops that their case did not
belong in the secular court. St Louis was able to forestall a decision because the citizens of Reims in the
meantime had rebelled against their bishop. The complicated case dragged on until 1248 when Louis left for the
crusade.

In the end St Louis won the war of nerves because of
his stubbornness and the papacy's abandonment of the
French bishops. Popes Gregory IX and Innocent IV
could not afford to offend the king since they needed
his help in their conflict with Frederick II. Revolts of
the French barons after 1235 against the church further
isolated the prelates. Moreover, the bishops concluded
that only the king had the power to enforce their inter-
dicts and excommunications. As the rebellious citizens
(bishops were frequently lords of cities) and episcopal
chapters ignored their bishops' spiritual anathemas
(which were overused), the prelates realized how dependent they were on the king's good grace.

Louis insisted that only he could decide when a
bishop's excommunication was justified, that is,
whether the bishop was using the sacred weapon for his
own political or monetary gain. St Louis claimed that
the king could punish his vassals (even if they were
bishops) when they violated the temporal rights of
others. In the Beauvais affair St Louis had always maintained that the church had no business in the dispute

since it was a feudal incident between lord and vassal
(the bishop was the king's vassal). To minimize clerical
opposition, moreover, St Louis sometimes interfered in
episcopal elections to ensure the choice of his own
candidates.

When Innocent IV was in Lyon St Louis refused to
recognize the pope's deposition and excommunication
of Frederick II. The French monarch received numerous
concessions from popes who needed the French in their
drive to retain political influence in Italy. As the popes
increased their taxation of the French clergy and dispensed French benefices to foreigners, the authority of
French bishops within their own dioceses decreased.
The widespread contempt of papal practices made the
French clergy turn to the monarch for protection. St
Louis experienced no pangs of conscience when he confiscated church resources in times of "necessity" (the
crusade, and the defense of the French realm from
attack). Besides, as the friars reminded him, should not
clerics live as the poor Christ? This evangelical criticism
of the higher clergy, a common refrain in the thirteenth
century, operated to the royal advantage.

NOBLES, BOURGEOISIE, PEASANTS

Unable to rebel against their suzerain after 1242, the
barons took out their aggressions on the church, on the
Muslims, on each other. They did not command the
financial resources to match the bulging treasury of the
king who could raise a large mercenary army at will. The
barons had difficulty controlling their own vassals and
towns. The rising cost of war and administration
reduced the military capability and economic status of
both magnates and petty nobles. St Louis' Parlement
kept the nobles off balance as lords learned to use the
nascent appellate court system to further their own
interests.

St Louis offended the great nobles. He denied the
peers the exclusive right to adjudicate their own dis-

putes, and outlawed the judicial duel and the wearing of arms in peacetime. The king was prone to fill royal offices with inferior nobles who were more loyal to the Capetian house than were the barons. Contrary to all custom St Louis jailed a great noble, Enguerran de Coucy. Louis was angered because Enguerran had hanged young nobles who were caught poaching on his land. St Louis shocked feudal society by unilaterally condemning him to death, a sentence later commuted to a fine and a promise to make a pilgrimage.

So too the towns were becoming isolated. Victimized by nobles and churchmen and torn by internal class conflicts, they were forced to rely on royal assistance. Gradually the king's intrusions into bourgeois administration and finance resulted in a subversion of urban liberties. St Louis multiplied extraordinary taxes on his towns primarily in order to finance his crusades.

The peasants revered St Louis who had a special care for his rural folk. When in 1250 the peasants around Paris learned of Louis' capture by the infidels in Egypt, they formed an army to rescue him. When this motly band turned to rioting in Paris and other cities Blanche reluctantly had them suppressed. The mystique of kingship was always strongest in the countryside where the king was considered a miracle-worker.

BLESSED ARE THE PEACEMAKERS

In 1259 Henry III finally gave up his claim to Normandy, Anjou, Maine, Touraine, and Poitou. In return, St Louis received liege homage from him for lands in southwestern France. Shortly thereafter, both the English king and his discontented barons asked St Louis to act as an arbiter in their quarrel. On numerous other occasions St Louis accepted invitations to settle disputes within and without the French kingdom. He arranged marriages and disputed territories involving Aragon and southern France. He settled the inheritance

of Flanders and Hainault. He established peace between
Navarre and Bar.

Prior to the reign of St Louis the papacy (or sometimes the emperor) often mediated international disputes. But beginning with Pope Gregory IX the papacy's
assault on the Hohenstaufen compromised its reputation
for impartiality. European powers therefore called upon
St Louis to do the job, a natural choice especially after
he attempted to adjudicate the conflict between Innocent IV and Frederick II. A mere king was refereeing a
fight between a pope and an emperor! When St Louis
departed on crusade and the pope continued his "crusade" against a Christian emperor, the French king's
international position was solidified.

The popes after 1250 shamelessly begged St Louis to
help them "regain" Sicily. Finally in 1266 the king permitted his brother, the ambitious Charles of Anjou, to
invade and conquer Sicily. In 1268 the last Hohenstaufen, Conradin, was publicly executed like a criminal. The result, however, was not papal hegemony in
Italy as might be expected, but a collapse of law and
order in that country. When the Sicilians expelled the
oppressive French in 1282 the popes frantically tried to
convince subsequent French kings (and other rulers in
Europe) to intervene in Sicily once more. A century of
Hohenstaufen-papal wars in Italy resulted in the harden-
ing of divisions within the communes and provinces of
Italy. The papal involvement in Italian affairs served to
retard Italy's political unification.

Charles of Anjou's unsuccessful attempt to build a
Mediterranean empire marked the end of medieval
universalist empires. The papal protégé, Charles, manipulated the papacy's weak condition for his own political aims. Although the church was far more centralized
institutionally in 1270 than in 1070, the pope behaved
more as a secular prince than the vicar of Christ. His
influence stemmed from his political power, not from
his holiness. By using the Roman church's spiritual

authority for political ends, the papacy sacrificed that authority. While St Louis lived, two French popes were elected; the number of French cardinals in the Curia increased, some of whom were Louis' former royal ministers. Europe had come full circle. The papacy in 1070 struggled to free itself from the German emperor. After two bitter centuries the papacy not only won this freedom, it even triumphed over its rival universalist power. But as a result the papacy found itself helplessly dependent on the king of France. What Gregory VII most dreaded had come to pass: the papacy at the mercy of a lay power. The balance of power in Christendom was shifting from Germany and Italy to France.

THE LAST CRUSADE

After 1254 St Louis' foreign policy was largely determined by his desire to head another crusade. But the barons were uninterested, and the prelates and towns feared the crushing royal taxes he levied for such purposes. By 1267 St Louis had finally amassed sufficient revenue to announce the new venture. For reasons not fully known, the king decided to capture Tunis before continuing on to the Holy Land. The heavily-armed crusaders, as usual ignorant of the terrain, arrived at the peak of the summer heat. St Louis' small army was decimated by dysentery, and he himself fell ill and died on 25 August 1270. Charles of Anjou ordered that his brother's bones be sent to St Denis near Paris and that the king's heart and intestines be buried in Palermo.

ST LOUIS CREATED CONDITIONS FOR THE "NATIONAL STATE"

Shortly after Louis IX died, Frenchmen began to speak of the golden age of St Louis, allegedly a time of peace, prosperity, and justice. Before the advent of Louis, the ideal ruler-type was Charlemagne; after 1270

kings were expected to emulate the legendary St Louis.
In the twentieth century, textbooks for French school
children refer to St Louis as a "patriotic" monarch or,
in some private schools, as a devout Catholic who governed a Catholic nation.

This fanciful and romantic version of St Louis and
his time makes modern historians weep. France in the
period 1226-1270 was in historical fact full of contradictions and turmoil. The rapid economic prosperity
was beneficial to many, it is true, but it occasioned
social dislocation and gross inequities. Particularly hard
hit were the knights who were victims of a more urbanized money economy. Moreover, crises of faith are
revealed in the proliferation of heresy. The secular
clergy resented the papal and royal privileges of the
friars. Each region had its own legal traditions, its own
tribunals. France was a hodgepodge of conflicting systems of law: customary feudal law, laws of the bourgeoisie and guilds, canon and civil law.

These legal tangles became acute as the barons attacked the clergy, the clergy and pope attacked the
barons, the barons encroached on their knights, the
pope pressured the prelates, and the royal officials made
inroads into towns and church lands. Since the pope was
involved elsewhere, these various groups appealed to the
monarch for protection. They were suspicious of the
king but they had no other choice. So desperately did
they require security and an arbiter that when their
rights were abrogated by royal officials they tended to
blame the officials, not the person of the king. They
wanted to believe in his purity.

None of these conditions were created by St Louis.
He inherited the largest and richest domain in the realm,
a domain which his royal ancestors had acquired largely
by force. St Louis had the more honorable task of
pacifying lands already held by the crown. He took advantage of the desire throughout France for order and
legal clarity. These remarks are not intended to belittle

the personal achievement of St Louis, but it must be emphasized that the peculiar socioeconomic and political conditions at the time made France receptive to the exercise of a single authority converging upon Paris. Local lords failed to realize that by calling upon the king and his Parlement to settle their differences they were undermining their own authority.

In 1100 the kingdom of the Franks was a collection of de facto independent regions with their own cultural and juridical traditions. The king's authority outside his own domanial lands was virtually nonexistent. It was impossible for nobles to form a "community of the realm" in opposition to royal power. By 1270 the king was learning how to divide and conquer the numerous principalities. St Louis laid the foundations for the first national state by: (1) providing all members of the kingdom with a single rallying point: the person (and to a lesser extent the office) of the king; (2) specializing certain departments of royal government for the purpose of efficient administration and tax collecting; (3) strengthening and, to some degree, centralizing the existing system of justice so that the king came to be seen as the font of justice in the realm. The king now had the instruments of power necessary to transform his exalted theoretical position into political fact. The king's person and his justice would eventually evolve into the vehicle which would unite the French people into a single political and cultural entity. After the fall of divine right monarchy in 1792 the trinity of industrialization, citizen army, and secularization of the church would complete the development of the nation state.

It would be simplistic to think of St Louis' "state" as the vanquisher of the "church." It would be more accurate to say that St Louis sanctified and legitimized the nascent French state, itself a sort of church. He believed that the temporal power (monarchy) and the spiritual power (church) were both necessary for man's salvation. The king helped the church defend the faith; he protected church lands and clerics. St Louis arrogated to himself many of the church's special concerns: care of the sick and the destitute, lepers, monasteries, heretics, Jews and other usurers, blasphemers, the crusade; he set an example of the ascetic and prayerful life. After centuries of trying to make the monarchy aware of its responsibilities to the church, the clergy discovered that they had done their job only too well. St Louis made monarchy a religion. To be sure, the concepts of "state" and "sovereign king" were meaningful only to a few. But a start had been made. The first step towards nationalism is the deification of the temporal power.

NATIONAL STATE: A PRODUCT OF THE PAPAL MONARCHY

Strangely, the universalist church was in large part the creator of the particularist state, especially in France. The papacy in 1095 initiated the crusade movement which was to elevate the dignity of French chivalry. King Louis IX of France presumed unilaterally to assume direction of two crusades. The heavy crusade taxes on towns and church lands imposed by St Louis set precedents for future levies; the extraordinary taxes would later become ordinary taxes. After Louis French kings would exploit the holy war idea for strictly political ends—thereby strengthening the crown's hold on the realm. Popes beginning from Innocent III gave French kings concession after concession in order to obtain French assistance against the Hohenstaufen enemy. The popes gave the French monarch the title Most Christian King. The crusade against the Cathars resulted in an expanded royal domain in southern France. Pope Gregory IX and his successors gave St Louis tacit permission to subordinate the French church to the crown.

The papal attack on the French barons threw them into
royal arms. Disillusioned with the papacy Frenchmen
took their grievances to the Parlement, thereby increasing the scope of royal justice. St Louis was asked to
arbitrate disputes. Under imperial pressure, the popes
looked the other way when French subjects complained
of the oppressive tactics of royal officials. St Louis
forced popes to consent to marriage alliances favorable
to the Capetians. Pontiffs permitted St Louis to assume
spiritual duties previously the primary concern of the
clergy. (A later pope consented to the canonization of
Louis IX, an act which elevated the Capetian line to
unparalleled heights.) By 1270 the king was the most
powerful single person in the kingdom of the Franks.

Thus the Gregorian papacy was instrumental in spiri-
tualizing a mere temporal king and in helping this king
increase control over his subjects, including the clergy.
Ironically the universalist pope became a common target
for every kind of hostility in France. The popes were
not, however, villains in this European drama. It is too
much to expect that human beings could resist the
temptation to use available means—the now streamlined
organizational papacy—to repel the brutal aggressions of
the Hohenstaufen. But the Gregorian papacy and the
Holy Roman Empire had gotten Europeans accustomed
to thinking in universalist terms. Hence when these two
monarchies depleted each other, Christians turned to
the French king, the nearest thing to an "emperor."

St Louis brought prophecy into government. This
charismatic monarch who acted like St Francis gave
politics a good name. The future was on the side of the
territorial state unified around a single symbol, a national monarch. Europe's fetish for social organization
eventually found an outlet in the sovereign state. "Thy
Kingdom come, thy will be done" was gradually being
transferred from the papacy and the empire to the
nation state.

CONCLUSIONS

By 1270 the Gregorian papacy and the Holy Roman Emperor were both incapable of providing a focal point for Christendom. The papacy had become overly dependent on the French king. The hope of a united Christendom began to wane.

St Louis' kingship had recovered the "spiritual" status lost by the emperors after the Investiture Controversy. The French monarchy no longer needed the church to give it religious respectability. The state under St Louis not only acted almost independently of the church, but it also commanded some of the church's material resources.

The French king by 1270 was the most powerful ruler in Europe. The balance of international power had shifted to France. Already the pacesetter in the visual arts and in learning, France was now assuming a kind of political leadership within Christendom.

St Louis, with the inadvertent help of Rome, laid the foundations for a French national state. The emergence of the national state in medieval France was in direct proportion to the progress of monarchical authority.

> *In attacking Boniface VIII, I have acted on behalf of God, the Roman church, the king, the kingdom, and my country.*
>
> William of Nogaret

V

THE SECOND REVOLUTION: PHILIP THE FAIR AND POPE BONIFACE VIII

St Louis' son, Philip the Bold (1270-1285), continued the policy of consolidating and expanding the royal domain. In 1282 the Sicilians expelled their French overlords and invited King Peter of Aragon to become their sovereign. After the long struggle to rid Sicily of the Hohenstaufen the popes were determined not to permit its loss so easily. Thus Pope Martin laid an interdict on Sicily, excommunicated Peter, and declared the throne of Aragon vacant. Martin then offered the crown to a son of Philip the Bold. Philip's "crusade" into Aragon, accompanied by a solemn papal promise of a plenary indulgence for all participants, proved a disaster for the French army. King Philip died of disease while making his retreat back to France in 1285.

The new king, Philip IV (1285-1314),* resolved never to engage in wild Mediterranean adventures and not to repeat another debacle like the Aragon crusade. Rather than fight the pope's battles, he would devote his energies to his own kingdom. His epoch-making clash with the papacy arose not out of an attempt to conquer Italian lands, but out of a desire to subdue Flanders and the French clergy.

Philip the Fair remains one of the most enigmatic figures in medieval history. Unlike his famous grandfather whose personality was frequently described by contemporaries, Philip the Fair's character and motives are cloudy. Perhaps Philip was unloved while he lived because his subjects were prone to compare him to the legendary St Louis. At any rate, Philip the Fair's habit of delegating authority to aggressive sometimes ruthless ministers makes it difficult for the historian to detect the precise extent of the king's will in any given governmental decision. While Philip the Fair may have occasionally given approval to plans drawn up by his advisors, he certainly gave continuous and forceful direction to the main course of his rule.

THE HERMIT POPE

When the papacy fell vacant in 1292 the twelve cardinals (six Roman, two French, four Italian) were deadlocked because of the antagonism between the three Colonnas and the three Orsini. Each of these two great Roman families desired the papal prize. When the plague

*The French called Philip IV the 'Fair," a reference not to his light complexion or sense of justice but to his handsomeness.

struck Rome the twelve continued their weary debates
at Perugia. Finally in July 1294 it was suggested that a
holy hermit, Peter of Morone, be elected pope. This
spectacular idea was at first resisted by the Orsini and
Colonna, but then Peter was a very old man and could
not be expected to live long. At least the deadlock
would be broken and, besides, the reputation of this
well-known monk would benefit the sagging prestige of
the papal name.

And so a legation was dispatched to the mountains to
inform the old hermit of the cardinals' decision. The
bewildered Peter of Morone was led not to Rome but to
Aquila. King Charles of Naples, who intended to keep
the new pope in his kingdom, immediately filled the
Curia with his nominees for cardinalships and benefices.
The simple hermit was given blank bulls to sign. Prelates
rushed to Naples to curry favor with Charles, the pope's
caretaker. The uncouth manner of this shaggy pontiff
scandalized the soft-living cardinals, but they soon
learned to use his impracticality to their advantage.

The advent of Pope Celestine V, the name Peter
adopted, brought great expectations throughout Christendom. At last a pure soul untainted by the world was
going to restore the papacy to its spiritual mission.
Especially hopeful were the literal adherents to St Francis' life of evangelical poverty, the Spiritual Franciscans,
who spoke of the coming of the Age of the Holy Spirit.
The spread of these unrealistic dreams led to discourage-
ment and cynicism when the dream was afterwards dis-
pelled. The hard work of structural reforms within the
church was retarded by the presence of this misplaced
prophet.

The reign of love was to last but six months. The
Curia's colossal administrative, financial, and diplomatic
machine made Celestine V nervous. Accordingly, on 13
December 1294 the harried pope mounted his throne
and announced his abdication. When he descended he
reclothed himself in his old rags and headed for his

beloved mountain cave. Ten days later the cardinals unanimously elected one of their own, Benedict Gaetani, who took the name Boniface VIII.

BONIFACE VIII (1294-1303)

Boniface VIII became pope in the worst of circumstances. Because many Christians expected Celestine to cure the ills of Christendom they felt cheated when he left. It was widely believed that Boniface persuaded Celestine to step down. Since Celestine's resignation was illegal (a pope had never resigned before), it was said, Boniface's election was likewise unlawful. When the joint armies of Charles of Naples and Boniface VIII captured Celestine as he tried to flee to Greece, Boniface had him incarcerated. The wild man died in his cell two months later, allegedly murdered by Boniface.

These mysterious circumstances surrounding Boniface VIII's election were to haunt him to the grave, and afterwards. Scion of a noble family near Rome Benedict Gaetani rose quickly in ecclesiastical circles before he. received the tiara. Something of his character is revealed in his rough handling of Parisian university professors over the question of mendicant rights to hear confessions. As papal legate to Paris, Cardinal Benedict in announcing his decision berated the masters as if they were schoolboys. Boniface's haughtiness and irascible temper would eventually precipitate his tragic downfall. As with most popes since Gregory VII Boniface was a canon lawyer with a lawyer's approach to church problems. He had a sound working knowledge of the papal bureaucracy and ran the daily affairs of the Curia with good professional sense. But Boniface VIII lacked the breadth of vision of an Innocent III. Even Boniface's friends (and they were few) agreed that there was nothing spiritual about him. He ran the church like a business. As frequently happens when a person of average intelligence and sensibility finds himself in high public office, Boniface became intoxicated with the power at his command. Unfortunately for the papacy Boniface confused his *image* of papalist supremacy with the real world of affairs. He did not realize that the Gregorian church could not be held together by force alone.

WAR BETWEEN FRANCE AND ENGLAND

While Boniface VIII was busy annulling Celestine's laws and firing the hermit's appointees, Philip the Fair and King Edward of England were each preparing a massive military and diplomatic effort over the duchy of Gascony. Edward complained that Philip the Fair was interfering with his rights in Gascony and fomenting a rebellion in Scotland. Philip was determined to assert his own rights in Gascony and break the English alliance with Flanders. To help finance the war both monarchs taxed their clergies without consulting the pope, a procedure which was formally illegal according to a canon proscribed by the Lateran Council of 1215. But since that date French and English kings had in practice kept a share of church taxes in return for their support of the pope's Italian policy. Because a secular government could not impose a subsidy on church lands for "secular" wars, it had to maintain the fiction that the revenue was to be used for religious purposes. Since neither king was a heretic, an infidel, or enemy of the pope, both kings had to argue that the war was necessary for national defense. When asked to contribute to the war effort, the clergy protested but in the end had to submit to royal pressure.

To stop the English-French conflict, Boniface VIII issued the bull *Clericis laicos* in February 1296 which forbade, under pain of excommunication, secular princes from taxing their clergy without papal consent; it also forbade the clergy, under pain of excommunication, from paying such subsidies to princes without Rome's approval. Technically the pope was within his rights to make such a request. Besides, was not the supreme pontiff the traditional arbiter of disputes among Christians? But the bull reveals how ignorant Boniface VIII was of political reality and how little he understood or cared about the widespread criticisms of papal policy. *Clericis laicos'* arrogant tone was hardly calculated to unite a divided Europe. It begins: "that laymen have been very hostile to the clergy antiquity relates. . . . For not content with what is their own the laity strive for what is forbidden. . . ." The bull categorically condemns all laymen and clergy who in any way participate in war subsidies unauthorized by the holy see. Did not Boniface VIII realize that the enforcement of this decree would have resulted in bloody internal conflicts within France and England? Did he actually believe that two of the most powerful kings in the West would stop their war at the pope's bidding? Did he not know that most Frenchmen and Englishmen, whatever their feelings about their kings and the war, resented such papal interference in their affairs? Popes at the time of St Louis were skillful in getting French support for their attacks on the Hohenstaufen; in return they gave tacit permission to the king to tax the French clergy—without raising issues of high principle. Boniface VIII's virtual declaration of war could only result in a humiliation for the pope.

To no one's surprise Philip the Fair and Edward I repudiated *Clericis laicos.* The embarrassed French clergy wrote to Boniface requesting that they be allowed to pay the subsidy to the crown. They told the pope how they were being branded traitors to their country and that they needed royal protection against the barons and townspeople. Weakening slightly, Boniface in September 1296 issued another bull *Ineffabilis amor* in which he admitted that the clergy could legitimately contribute for the defense of the realm. Chastising "his son" Philip, Boniface interpreted Philip the Fair's recent decree to forbid the export of gold and silver from the

French kingdom—thus cutting off the flow of revenue to Rome—as directed against him.

BONIFACE VIII CAPITULATES

Boniface in 1296 was enmeshed in Italian politics. Although on relatively good terms with the Colonna family before his election he ignored the Colonnas in his subsequent distribution of favors. When Boniface interfered in the domestic affairs of Sciarra Colonna the latter retaliated by seizing a convoy of papal treasure on the road from Anagni. Boniface deprived the Colonna cardinals of their benefices and confiscated their property. The Colonnas withdrew into the castle of Longhezza where they were joined by leaders of the Spiritual Franciscans who hated Boniface for declaring them heretical and for allegedly depriving them of their revered Celestine. From this fortress the Colonnas issued manifestoes in which they denied the legality of Celestine's renunciation and therefore of Boniface VIII's election, accused Boniface of using church goods for personal gain, and called for a general church council to elect a new pope.

As the civil war between the Gaetani and the Colonna worsened, Boniface VIII was forced to bend to the king of France. The pope was also burdened by delicate negotiations he was conducting in both Germany and Sicily. Hence in July 1297 Boniface issued *Esti De Statu* which explicitly gave Philip the Fair permission to tax his clergy for the "defense of the realm" *without* prior papal approval. Philip alone could decide when such a state of national emergency existed. Boniface could no longer afford to do without revenue from the French church while he fought the Colonna in Italy. As an additional favor to Philip the Fair Boniface canonized Louis IX in the same year—an act which had the effect of making Philip's wars seem "religious."

Released from French and English distractions Boniface devoted his energy against the Colonnas. He preached a "crusade" against them, excommunicated them to the fourth generation, seized their property and turned much of it over to his own Gaetani family. Boniface had the town of Palestrina, a Colonna refuge, leveled to the ground and had the site ploughed with salt. By 1299 papal troops had crushed the Colonna clan. But the price of victory was perhaps too steep. For while Boniface had consolidated Gaetani power in and around Rome, he sacrificed much of the prestige of St Peter. Europe complained that the money siphoned off to Rome was being used to finance the pope's private feuds. The exiled Colonnas formed a conspiracy network which propagandized the supposed illegality of Boniface's election and the need for a general council. Boniface's crusade against the Colonnas made the latter's case seem only too plausible. A Colonna clique in Paris was in contact with the university and the royal court. Philip the Fair's stature was enhanced when he resisted an unpopular pope, and the pope backed down. But *Esti De Statu* was not only a moral triumph for Philip the Fair, it strengthened his military arm. The French clergy found it even harder to resist forthcoming royal demands for "contributions."

Boniface VIII was further humiliated by the refusal of France and England to permit him to arbitrate their dispute. Finally Philip the Fair and Edward allowed Benedict Gaetani, as a "private person" not as pope, to settle the matter. A series of marriage alliances in 1298 between the English and French royal houses was to cement the peace. Some of Philip's advisors were grieved that their king did not demand the annexation of Gascony into the royal domain. But the conservative Philip preferred to continue the gradual encroachment of royal justice into the duchy with an eye to future annexations. With Flanders Philip was less gentle. The defeated Count Guy of Flanders found himself in a royal dungeon and his fief confiscated. For the remainder of his reign Philip the Fair engaged his full resources in pursuit of the conquest of the prosperous Flemish county.

By 1300 Boniface VIII had lulled himself into believing that the traditional French-papal détente had been restored. But the basic issues were in fact unresolved. Did the pope have the right to influence secular politics in France? Did the pope have the unilateral right to interfere in French ecclesiastical affairs? Could he prevent the king from taxing the clergy? To put it another way, were the French clergy an intrinsic part of the body politic of France or did they form a legal enclave beyond the reach of royal justice?

JUBILEE OF 1300

Throughout the years 1294-1300 Boniface VIII was taken up with the humdrum activities of supervising the vast curial administration. If one overlooks his misguided meddling in French and English tax questions and his vendetta against the Colonna, it must be said that Boniface was a fair-minded and able administrator. For many he was a welcome relief following the Celestinian circus. Boniface drew up a set of decretals and took steps to centralize the church in the papacy. He settled European disputes and rooted out local church abuses.

His approach to the papacy is well illustrated by his handling of the friars. A partisan of the mendicants before his election, Boniface as pope promulgated a bull in 1300 which restricted their rights to hear confessions, preach, and collect burial fees. By these restrictions Boniface hoped to lessen the friction between the friars and the secular priests, and to have the two groups work in harmony for the good of the church universal. Previous popes had too often exploited mendicant services to obtain their own immediate goals. Boniface continued to seek their services but he also subordinated them to the episcopate in the interests of efficiency. Characteristically Boniface saw the mendicant orders as an administrative problem. The thought of using the holy men in an effort to raise the spiritual level of the church was foreign to his thinking. But while Boniface sought to incorporate the mendicant orders more fully into the institutional structure of the church, at the same time he gave individual friars numerous concessions and appointed some eighty Dominicans and Franciscans to episcopal sees. To contemporaries this dual policy seemed ambiguous. As a result this attempt at compromise satisfied neither the friars nor the seculars.

In 1300 Boniface VIII proclaimed a jubilee. Any pilgrim who visited the basilicas in Rome was promised full pardon of his sins—a privilege usually granted only to crusaders. Vast groups of Christians streamed into the eternal city. Boniface interpreted this display of Christian piety as a manifestation of faith in the papacy. Let the Colonna say what they may about his supposed illegitimacy, this clear mandate from God's children was for Boniface proof that he was true pope and that his policies were from on high. During this year of celebration Boniface seems to have deluded himself into thinking that the canonist doctrine of the pope's "fullness of power" was a realized fact. Accordingly he hatched new schemes for further encroachments of Gaetani power into the Patrimony, Florence, Sicily, and Germany.

THE SAISSET AFFAIR

In the early 1290s Bernard Saisset, abbot of a monastery in Pamiers in southern France, quarrelled with the local count over jurisdictional rights in the town of Pamiers. The count settled the issue by ejecting the abbot from his monastery. Saisset appealed his case to Boniface VIII who ruled in his favor. Seeking to expand papal rights in Languedoc, the pope even carved

out a new bishopric at the expense of the bishop of
Toulouse and named Saisset its first bishop.

Saisset was a vulgar sort of person who usually alienated everyone with whom he came in contact. A local
patriot, he publicly criticized the behavior of
"French" (from near Paris) royal officials and even the
person of the king. During one of his many conflicts
with Toulouse the bishop of that city denounced Saisset
to the king in 1301. Philip the Fair used this opportunity to increase his control over the Inquisition in the
area and over the church in Languedoc. The monarch
ordered a secret inquest and sent in his agents who immediately seized Saisset's goods and dragged his servants
off to prison. The shaken bishop appealed to his metro-
politan, the archbishop of Narbonne, who complained
to the king. Philip as usual apologized for the excesses
of his agents and ordered Saisset brought to Paris. As
Philip sat listening to the ramblings of this obnoxious
southerner he must have realized that it would be an
easy matter to isolate diplomatically so unpopular a
bishop. Afterwards Saisset remarked, in one of the rare
reported descriptions of Philip the Fair, "Our king
resembles an owl, the fairest of birds, but worthless. He
is the handsomest man in the world but he only knows
how to stare at people unblinking, in silence. He is
neither a man nor a beast; he is a statue."

Philip the Fair summoned his court before an assembly of bishops in Senlis to announce charges against
Saisset. Philip observed while his minister, Pierre Flote,
shouted out accusations: Saisset denounced the king's
debased coinage, called the king a bastard, poked fun at
Pierre Flote's physical defect (he had one eye), sold
church offices, uttered blasphemies, and behaved like a
heretic and a traitor. The startled bishops became aware
that the king brought them to Senlis not to try a dissident bishop, but to be browbeaten into accepting a
royal attack on certain ecclesiastical jurisdictions in Lan-

guedoc. This bizarre "trial" was a beautifully orchestrated show in which the prelates were being trapped into doing the king's dirty work. It was a performance which could never have happened under St Louis.

In the charged emotional atmosphere of the trial there were cries of, "Kill him on the spot." But the archbishop of Narbonne rescued Saisset by urging that Saisset be permitted to appeal to Rome. Forced to concede to the archbishop, Philip the Fair had Saisset imprisoned in the jail of the bishop of Senlis, a personal friend of the king. The king quickly dashed off the list of fantastic accusations to the Curia and brashly demanded that Boniface VIII condemn Saisset and deprive him of his clerical status. To the list Philip added that Saisset affirmed "that our very Holy Father Boniface is the devil incarnate, and against all truth and justice he had canonized St Louis, who is on the contrary in hell."

Philip the Fair was confident that Boniface would give in again over the taxation of the clergy as he had in 1297. Philip felt that the pope was enough of a political realist to know that Saisset's fate was already sealed; the southern bishops had reconciled themselves to Saisset's fall. A nod from the pope was all that was left. The king knew of the pressures on Boniface from the Colonna and other dissidents in Rome. Besides, was not Charles of Valois, Philip's brother, negotiating with the pope for a future French expedition to Sicily?

But Boniface VIII stood firm. If a king were permitted to jail ecclesiastics on trumped up charges, what would become of the church's liberties? Boniface had the force of canon law and tradition behind him. It was illegal for a prince to interfere in ecclesiastical justice. A criminal cleric was to be judged by the church not the state. If secular rulers were permitted to violate ecclesiastical persons and their property, the church would be reduced to the handmaiden of the prince and would be unable to perform its function of saving souls. But unfortunately for the papacy Boniface, surrounded by self-serving bureaucrats who shielded him from unpleasant reality, miscalculated the strength of the French monarchy and misunderstood the realignment of sociopolitical forces which had been slowly occurring in France since St Louis. Boniface VIII tried to make actual political conditions conform to his legalistic conceptions of what he fancied the church should be. Philip the Fair tried to make legal principles conform to his specific actions regarding the church; if the law failed to catch up with his acts, so much the worse for the law. In this ensuing clash the papal protégé from Pamiers was quickly forgotten by both sides.

THE POPE AND A MERE KING, (1301-1303)

Boniface overreacted to Philip the Fair's demands. He insisted that Saisset's impounded goods be restored and that the bishop be allowed to come to Rome. Two days later (7 December 1301) the Gaetani pope revoked the concessions conceded to Philip in 1297 and forbade French prelates to pay subsidies without papal permission. About the same time, he drew up the bull *Ausculta, Fili Carissime* (Listen, most beloved son) in which he assumes the posture of a father reprimanding a naughty child. Boniface reminds the king that he is "subject" to the holy see. Philip confers benefices without consulting the pope. He tries churchmen in his own courts, not in ecclesiastical tribunals. He unjustly steals church revenues for his own uses. Boniface terms Philip a "degenerate son of illustrious forebears," a not so subtle allusion to St Louis. Finally the pope summons the churchmen of France to meet in Rome on 1 November 1302 to decide "what shall seem fitting for the reform of the above-mentioned matters and for your guidance and peace and health and for good government in your realm." Philip is requested to appear in person, but the synod would if necessary proceed without him. This last is nothing less than a threat of excommunication and deposition.

Something like *Ausculta* could have been written by Gregory IX or Innocent IV when these pontiffs were attempting to drive the Hohenstaufen out of Italy. But Philip the Fair was in France not Italy. He never had serious designs in Italy. Boniface VIII played European politics in the manner of a military commander pushing toy guns on a cardboard map. Boniface's provocative gesture may have been canonically correct, but it was political lunacy. By this irresponsible challenge to Philip the Fair Boniface shattered the traditional alliance between Paris and Rome, an alliance now so necessary for the papacy's lifeblood.

The bull *Ausculta* was burned in Paris, by whom is not known. In its place Philip the Fair's agents concocted and circulated a crude forgery in which Boniface is supposed to have said that the French king is subject to the pope "in spirituals and temporals." Another forgery purporting to be Philip's reply began, "Philip, by the grace of God king of the French, to Boniface who acts as though he were pope, little or no greeting. Let your great fatuity know that in temporals we are subject to no one; that the collations of vacant churches and prebends belong to us by royal right and that their revenues are ours. . . . All who think otherwise we account fools and madmen. Given at Paris."

Philip the Fair reacted violently to the papal attack. In April 1302 he summoned a meeting of clergy, nobles, and bourgeoisie to Notre Dame cathedral in Paris—the first assembly of its kind in French history. From the pulpit Pierre Flote harangued the crowd with a thundering blast against the "heretic" in Rome. Boniface, claimed Flote, accounted the king as his feudal vassal (an idea taken from the above-mentioned forged bull). Boniface filled the French church with foreigners, non-residents who stole from the poor. The French must protect themselves from Roman greed.

Following Flote's diatribe someone suggested that each of the three groups pen a letter to Boniface. The nobles hurried off a vehement letter to the college of cardinals—not to the pontiff. In bombastic language they urged the cardinals to support them against the so-called pope. The letter of the townspeople to the cardinals has not survived. The clergy, embarrassed and confused, meekly asked the king for permission to attend the pope's council in November. The king's ministers curtly informed them they had to make a choice between king and pope; to go to Rome was an act of disloyalty to the kingdom. The clergy then wrote a respectful letter to Boniface relating the charges made in Notre Dame. Pretending not to know that the circulating bull was a phony, the clerics feigned surprise that Boniface had claimed feudal overlordship over their monarch. They ended by begging the pope not to compel them to attend the November council in Rome for fear that they would incite Philip's wrath. The prelates lamented that no one in France obeyed their spiritual censures, the people were on the verge of pillaging the church, and they the clergy were everywhere branded traitors to the king. If they went to Rome, pleaded the clergy, the French church would be in jeopardy.

With this assembly Philip recovered the initiative. What had started as Philip's provocative offensive against the church (Bishop Saisset) ended as a supposed defense of himself and his realm. Philip had succeeded in making it appear as if Boniface were the real aggressor.

Boniface rejected the French clergy's request not to come to Rome and reproached them for their weakness. The cardinals, for their part, refused to side with the nobles and the commons. They deemed it more prudent to declare, at least verbally, for the Roman pontiff. Philip had overestimated his influence in the Curia.

On the morning of 17 May 1302 the citizens of Bruges butchered the resident French garrison. As the

revolt against French domination spread throughout
Flanders, Philip the Fair mobilized his army and
marched to the northeast. In July the invading French
force was wiped out at Courtrai. Europe was stunned at
the news of lowborn townspeople inflicting such a
defeat on the finest of French chivalry. Among those
who celebrated the Flemish victory was Boniface VIII
who proclaimed it a judgment of God. For not only was
a disobedient king punished, but the antipapal minister
Pierre Flote was killed in the battle.

Seething with revenge Philip the Fair personally led
into Flanders another fruitless expedition. His reputation slightly tarnished, Philip was forced to lower his
tax-rates (for a renewed Flemish invasion) and wait for
the results of the papal council in November. At this
council 36 of the 78 French bishops appeared—none
from the north of France. The northern bishops, traditionally allied to the crown, defied the papal call in the
interests of political expediency. Frustrated by the (36)
bishops' unwillingness to condemn their king, Boniface
VIII on 18 November 1302 drew up *Unam Sanctam*,
perhaps the most well-known papal bull of the middle
ages.

Unam Sanctam makes no reference to Philip the Fair.
Rather, it strings together quotes and paraphrases from
Scripture and theological authorities. The bull opens
". . . there is one holy, Catholic and apostolic
church . . . outside this church there is no salvation. . . ." In this church there are two swords, spiritual
and temporal. The former is exercised by the priest, the
latter by kings and soldiers, "though at the will . . . of
the priest." If the earthly power shall err, "it shall be
judged by God alone and not by man. . . . We therefore
declare, state, define, and pronounce that it is altogether
necessary to salvation for every human creature to be
subject to the Roman Pontiff."

Philip and his advisors must have interpreted *Unam
Sanctam* as nothing less than a papal claim to direct

interference in French politics, ecclesiastical and secular. This view was reinforced when Boniface sent a papal nuncio to Philip with an ultimatum. Philip must release all his bishops to come to Rome, recognize the pope's right to appoint bishops and grant clerical privileges, permit the pope to send legates to settle any dispute, agree not to seize church property and the goods of bishoprics during vacancies. Philip was being commanded to abandon his hold on the French church. Still smarting from his thrashing in Flanders Philip equivocated his replies. Not satisfied with the king's response Boniface on 13 April 1303 directed his nuncio to announce publicly the excommunication of the king of France. At that, Boniface VIII's word game was ended. The papacy had signed its own death warrant.

The Saisset episode triggered royalists and papalists to establish a theoretical foundation for the actions of Philip the Fair and Boniface VIII respectively. This third great pamphlet war of the middle ages—following the Investiture Controversy and the Frederick II-Innocent IV conflict—is particularly significant because it catapulted the secular state to respectability.

THE PAPALISTS SPEAK

The papalist writers build their case on the church's unity. Christ's earthly kingdom is one and is headed by Christ's vicar. The organization of the church is deduced from the principle that the spiritual is superior to the temporal, the heavenly to the earthly, the supernatural to the natural. Since the priest is intrinsically superior to the layman, the former has ultimate authority in questions of property and secular politics. It follows that the priest, par excellence the pope, can sometimes interfere in secular government especially if "sin" is involved.

Perhaps the most extreme of these papalists was Egidius Romanus who wrote *On Ecclesiastical Power* in 1302. In this treatise Egidius multiplied the number of special cases in which the pope could intervene in temporal affairs and in local church matters. The pope "permits" secular rulers to govern, provided of course that they are good Catholics and subservient to the First Apostle. Not wanting to appear out-of-fashion, Egidius did not blindly appeal to tradition, but he logically constructed his elaborate system upon the latest Aristotelian and theological studies. His ponderous tract is a monument to consistency—but wholly irrelevant. Ignoring the specific issues of the Philip-Boniface conflict, Egidius seems to absolutize church structure for its own sake. Egidius' utopian church—static, hierarchical, efficient—existed only in his mind. His treaties had no impact on the course of events in Europe at the time or afterwards. Unable to convince anyone but the most staunch papal devotees, Egidius probably had difficulty getting even his friends in the Curia to read his formidable tome.

In general the papalist writers greatly expanded the pope's theoretical power. While they gaily drew out the implications in the "fullness of power" inherent in the papacy, they seemed oblivious to the pope's actual influence in European politics, an influence which had been declining for the past fifty years. Is the society portrayed in these treatises the fulfillment of the Gregorian dream? Yes, in the sense that Gregory VII wanted to centralize the church under the papacy, and to make the clergy a separate juridical class. No, in that Gregory VII would not have approved of such excessive influence in secular politics and local church affairs. Above all, Gregory would have been horrified by the legalism which pervaded these papalist tracts, and by the absence of prophetic leadership—in theory as well as in fact. Egidius Romanus cared nothing for the idea of an aggressive reformist pope who would use his office to evangelize society. The papalists wanted to preserve the present system, not change it. Gregory VII was a revolutionary, Boniface VIII a reactionary.

What Boniface VIII's loyalists never comprehended was that their arduous attempts to construct abstract models would never win converts to the papal cause. Boniface did not need academic arguments, but rather a type of propaganda which was aimed at people's real fears and hopes. It is a sad commentary on the mental state of the pope that in the midst of this crisis his only response was to harken back to the need for unity in the church. Given the dubious political policies of recent popes, somehow Boniface VIII's appeals for faith in the system and for near absolute power rang hollow.

THE ROYALISTS RESPOND

The salvos of Egidius and other papalists put French monarchists on the defensive, for no one in 1300 would have denied that the spiritual was superior to the temporal, nor that the pope was the spiritual head of one Catholic church. Never having engaged the pope so fiercely in the past, the French had little polemic tradition to draw upon. Hence compared to the papalists the royalist replies are more diverse. Rather than attempt to build logical systems of thought, they generally barrage their readers with bald proroyal and antipapal assertions.

The king's pamphleteers use two lines of defense. First, they contend that temporal affairs (politics, royal justice, property, money, war) are the king's business, no one else's. God ordained that in His church the king (and other secular rulers) should care for the temporal needs of Christians, the clergy the spiritual. The king and the pope should each keep to his own proper sphere of action. Philip the Fair's publicists support this two power theory with arguments from Scripture, theology, Roman and canon law (did not Innocent III say that the king of France had no superior in temporals?), Aristotle, history. Some typical propositions: Old Testament kings had power over priests; according to the Roman right of

prescription anyone who holds property unmolested for
a period of time becomes the legal owner of that property (therefore the French realm belongs to the king);
since Christ rejected a temporal kingdom, it follows that
Christ's delegate, the pope, has no temporal jurisdiction
(outside the Papal States).

But this first line of defense had weaknesses. The
royalists were forced to admit that the pope could intervene in the king's affairs at least in some instances; they
could only insist that in this particular instance Pope
Boniface had overstepped his authority. Surely, retorted
the papalists, in the interests of church unity the king's
interests should be subordinate to the pope's interest in
saving souls. Surely the church is the ultimate interpreter of the Bible. If the king is the supreme overlord
in temporals, by what right does he interfere in church
matters (taxing clergy, jailing and restraining bishops,
resisting a pope, ignoring excommunications, punishing
heretics and Jews)? The royalists had trapped themselves in a corner.

The second line of defense was even harder to support. Philip's publicists held that the king had some
rights in spiritual matters. After all, the king, no mere
layman, belongs to a family distinguished for its Christian virtue. Witness Charlemagne* and St Louis. Capetian monarchs have traditionally protected the church
and the faith, led crusades, governed a realm renowned
for its holy priests. (Philip the Fair was merely repeating
those arguments traditionally echoed by the French
clergy in order to persuade the king to watch over their
interests.) Moreover, the consecrated king had the supernatural power to cure the skin disease scrofula.

But the papalists shot back: granted the king's spiritual rights, where did he get them? The *clergy* canonized
St Louis and anointed French kings. Despite his status

*The Capetians encouraged the false legend that Charlemagne was
one of their ancestors.

the king is not a priest. He neither preaches the Word nor dispenses the sacraments. Hence what the church gives it can take away. Since the pope is the highest priest he can dethrone unworthy kings.

The most sophisticated royalist reply came from a Dominican theologian, John of Paris, who synthesized both lines of defense. He demonstrated that it was possible to have a separation of powers—king in temporals, pope in spirituals—while preserving the unity of Christendom. John also showed that the king had a legitimate interest in souls because he had the obligation to lead men to "natural' virtue. John of Paris fabricated his elaborate two power system for a practical end: the deposition of a pope. While seeming to present a balanced theory which gives equal powers to both king and pope, he actually wanted to show that it was legitimate and virtuous for a king to persuade a general church council to oust a pope for the crimes of promoting heresy, destroying the church, and stirring up rebellion in a kingdom—exactly those charges that French royalists were bringing against Boniface VIII.

THE KING'S DILEMMA

But while John of Paris' political philosophy might have satisfied Parisian intellectuals it was too subtle to be of much help to the king. Uninterested in theological correctness Philip needed a practical weapon designed to extract revenues from the clergy and to rouse his people against his enemy in Rome. Protests against the government's moves had to be drowned out in a bombardment of inflammatory catchphrases. Yet his clerical taxes and his resistance to the Holy Father had to appear conservative and just. Here the publicists were successful. They gave him the key: the idea of extraordinary jurisdiction.

The king resolved his dilemma by appealing to the necessity to "defend the realm." Philip was "reluc-

tantly" driven to tax everyone in the realm—including
even the clergy who were *ordinarily* exempt—in the face
of English and Flemish "aggressions." All privileges and
liberties were suspended for the duration of the national
emergency. Philip denied that he was turning the crusade tax into a tax for political ends. (Unlike modern
Americans no Frenchman in 1300 believed that the central government had the right to tax its subjects for the
ordinary expenses of running a government.) Philip
insisted that he levied these extraordinary taxes for "religious" wars against God's enemies. Any means was
justified, he claimed, to repel a threat to national security. Surely anyone who refused to contribute to so
noble a cause was committing a mortal sin.

ROYALIST PROPAGANDA IN ACTION

An example of how this "defense of the realm" idea
worked can be seen in a sermon preached in Paris, 1302,
on the eve of the king's invasion of Flanders. The
(anonymous) priest proclaimed that anyone who died in
battle against the wicked Flemish was assured a martyr's
crown in heaven! To die for the king and for the kingdom was the equivalent of dying at the hands of the
infidel in the Holy Land. Whoever wages war against the
king of France is an enemy of Justice and the Catholic
church. Everyone in the realm must contribute—with
money if he is not disposed to fight in person—to this
holy war. France is God's special concern and must not
fall to the devil.

The preacher of this astonishing sermon may have
had his theology twisted, but he knew how to sell war.
He bulldozed his listeners with concepts which asso-
ciate, however haphazardly, the coming war to all that
men at the time professed to be sacred: Christ, church,
crusade. Not to respond to the royal bugle was alleged
to be treason against God and king. It is not recorded
how the preacher explained the subsequent defeat of
the French at Courtrai.

In early 1303 Philip the Fair launched his all out attack on Boniface VIII. Encouraged by the success of the last assembly the king summoned two assemblies of his magnates, clergy, and townsmen. At these meetings royal ministers screamed out their abuse on Boniface who was accused of heresy, blasphemy, sodomy, witchcraft, adultery, etc. Boniface does not believe in the immortality of the soul, it was charged, because he once said that he would rather be a dog than a Frenchman. Since everyone knows that a dog does not possess a soul Boniface's statement is clearly heretical. Boniface had Celestine V killed in prison. Boniface claimed that fornication is no more a sin that rubbing one's hands together. The only way to save our holy kingdom and the Catholic church, cried the king's men, is to summon a general council and have this pseudo-pope deposed.

The leader of this rhetorical assault on Boniface was the minister William of Nogaret, a lawyer from southern France. Rather than reply point by point to *Unam Sanctam* and Egidius' abstruse argumentation, Nogaret appealed instead to the *emotions* of Frenchmen. His task was to galvanize public opinion against the person of Boniface VIII and divert the people's attention away from the king's defeat at Courtrai. Nogaret attacked not the institution of the papacy, but the person of the pope. He skillfully exploited French grievances against Boniface and his nuncios.

William of Nogaret was a virtuoso in the fine art of propaganda. He proudly proclaimed that he was ready to die for his king, his kingdom, his *patria* or fatherland. At the time the French word *pays* usually referred to the immediate locality where one was born. From Roman law Nogaret borrowed the idea of Rome as the common *patria* and applied it to the entire kingdom of France. It is the duty of all, said Nogaret, to come to the aid of the common *pays*, the kingdom. He declared that the French kingdom was a sort of single *patria*, a "country" to which all inhabitants owe ultimate allegiance. He also told the French that they were the "chosen people" favored by God above all other races. In effect Nogaret claimed that to support the king's "defensive" war against the pope was to defend France, the king, the church, the Catholic faith. A later propaganda artist, Adolf Hitler, would say that if you must tell a lie, tell a big one—and repeat it unceasingly.

William of Nogaret did not point to theory but to expediency. Since the pope was destroying France and the universal church, warned Nogaret, someone must rid the church of this cancer. Afterwards some willing and able Christian ruler must assume (at least temporarily) those responsibilities neglected by the pope. In the crisis atmosphere of the time Nogaret's appeal to the job-yet-to-be-done was more effective than rational argument. Any discussion of the legality of the king's claim to extraordinary jurisdiction, he implied, would be sacrilegious since nothing less than the existence of the church and the realm was at stake. This was not a time for talk but for action.

It must be noted that for Philip the Fair the tangle with Boniface was secondary to his ongoing involvement in Flanders. Boniface VIII was a convenient stalking horse which was useful in terrorizing the clergy into making contributions for Philip's Flemish campaigns. In the two-front war on Flanders and Rome the French monarchy emerged the winner.

Is this to imply that all Frenchmen in 1300 were "nationalists" and willing to die in battle for "France"? Of course not, otherwise the king would not have had to resort to extensive propaganda. It would take centuries for sectional patriotism (derived from the word *patria*) to diminish. But Philip the Fair had convinced at least some people that loyalty to the king and the territory of France preceded loyalty to the pope. St Louis gave a religious face to the monarchy and built up the instruments of royal power. Philip the Fair extended the religious image of the monarchy to include the French nation, its people and its land. For Philip's advisors the most appropriate manifestation of national sentiment was the sacrifice of one's life on the battlefield. It is no coincidence that in the twentieth century national governments have made extensive use of their propaganda apparatuses during wartime. The chief differences between twentieth-century nationalism and its fourteenth-century predecessor are that modern governments have greater police and tax powers, that virtually *all* modern citizens are devout nationalists (Philip the Fair could muster only a few true believers; the rest went along only for the moment), and that the modern nation state is itself a religion, a sort of deity without God. In 1300 even Nogaret would have conceded that God and the church required a Christian's absolute devotion.

ANAGNI

When Philip the Fair learned that Boniface VIII was going to tack a bull of excommunication on the cathedral door in Anagni on 8 September 1303, he dispatched Nogaret to arrest Boniface and take him to Paris. With the help of Italian mercenaries Nogaret and Sciarra Colonna attacked the town of Anagni at dawn, 7 September. They found traitors in Anagni, Boniface's birthplace, to open the gates. As they marched to the papal palace the urban militia did not resist the invaders. Most of the cardinals fled while Boniface's nephews elected to defend the palace. After some fighting the attackers broke into Boniface's chamber and found him, according to one account, clad in full regalia seated on his throne. Sciarra wanted to kill him immediately but Nogaret held his hand. Boniface was kept prisoner while Nogaret bargained with the pope's Italian enemies to let him take the criminal back to France where he would be tried by a general council. During this respite the citizens of Anagni had a change of heart. They ousted the

besiegers and released the pope who then returned to
Rome. But the nightmare of Anagni was too much for
the aged pontiff. On 12 October 1303 Boniface VIII
was found dead in his bed.

The outrage at Anagni disgusted most Christians.
Even Dante, no friend of Boniface, was shocked by this
savage assault on the pope's person. But in France there
were no public demonstrations against the sacrilege.
Without implicating Philip, Boniface's successor promptly excommunicated Nogaret who responded by writing
a lengthy justification for his actions. Nogaret explained
that he had "acted legitimately and with a praiseworthy
zeal for God, the faith, and the defense of the holy
church of God, and especially for his lord the king and
for the kingdom of France which Boniface, as their
perfidious enemy, persecuted." In combatting Boniface
Nogaret had acted on behalf of "justice, the Roman
church, the public good . . . the kingdom, and his country (patria)." It is doubtful that anyone believed Nogaret's apology, but he deftly made the royal affront
appear an act of self-defense. Nogaret in effect was in-
structing his government on the proper way to rationalize future raids on church liberties.

PHILIP THE FAIR'S TOTAL VICTORY

No government adept in the use of propaganda willingly abandons an enemy which can serve as an object
of hostility. Nothing unites better than hate. Philip the
Fair would not let Boniface VIII escape so easily. He
found that it was less difficult to get his people to vent
their aggressions upon a bad pope than upon the Flemish. His "we" (the French) needed a "they" (Boniface
and his allies). Just as a Roman faction in 896 had sat in
judgment upon a dead pope (the rotting corpse was
dragged from the grave for this purpose), so Philip the
Fair hounded Boniface VIII even in death. Philip succeeded in pressuring the new pope, Benedict XI, into

overturning all of Boniface's sentences against him, the king. Still unsatisfied, Philip bullied Benedict's successor, the Frenchman Clement V (1305-14), into starting an investigation into the life and beliefs of the late Boniface VIII. Nogaret compiled a long list of accusations against his adversary's ghost. If Philip could get the pope to nullify Boniface's election and declare him a heretic, the crown's hold over the French clergy would be tightened.

The macabre trial of Boniface began in 1310. Boniface's opponents flocked to Avignon to offer testimony, much of which was as exaggerated as the accusations hurled by Nogaret and the Colonnas. Pope Clement expunged from the records all acts of Boniface which Philip found offensive. The pope lifted Nogaret's excommunication. He even congratulated Philip for praiseworthy zeal in attacking Boniface and defending the church! As a final concession Clement V had Peter Morone, the hermit pope, canonized a saint.

But although Philip the Fair and his agents were thoroughly vindicated, Boniface VIII, oddly, was not formally condemned. At the final moment in the trial Philip discovered that he needed Pope Clement in his attack on the Templars. He decided that it was enough that he the king was restored in his dignity and in those rights usurped by Boniface whose memory was forever tainted with evil suggestion.

The victory over Boniface VIII spurred Philip on to more daring feats. Out of desire to seize the revenue and property of the Knights Templar, a military religious order such as the one founded by St Bernard, Philip instructed Nogaret to plan the destruction of the Templars. After two years of preparation Philip in 1307 got Clement to order an investigation of the Templars' alleged crimes of heresy and immorality. The king had all Templars in France imprisoned and put to the most brutal kinds of mental and physical torture. In what may be the first recorded instance of mass brainwashing the Templars publicly confessed to sordid offenses: spitting on the crucifix, kissing a cat's behind during the initiation ceremony, etc. At large assemblies of the realm Philip's henchmen whipped up a popular furor against the Templars and even against Clement who was accused of not moving fast enough in the proceedings. In 1312 Clement had the order suppressed. Two years later the Grand Master of the Templars was burned at the stake in Paris.

Philip's greatest coup was in getting the popes to remain in the kingdom of France. Clement V, former archbishop of Bordeaux, was crowned in Lyon on his way to Rome. But when told of disorders in Italy Clement decided to stay temporarily in France. In 1309 Clement settled in the town of Avignon, technically a part of the empire but actually French in culture. Of the 28 cardinals Clement created, 25 were French—giving the French a majority in the college. From 1309 to 1377 the popes, all French, lived at Avignon. It was widely believed that the popes were puppets of the king of France. The scandal of the Babylonian Captivity, as the papal residence in Avignon was sometimes called, dealt a severe blow to the prestige of the papacy. It was axiomatic for all Christians that the pope belonged in Rome, burial ground of the first pope and the spiritual hub of Christendom.

END OF THE GREGORIAN PROMISE

The twin catastrophe of Anagni and Avignon dismembered the medieval papal monarchy. The Avignon papacy, although still able to command money and benefices, was a lifeless shell. (It is perhaps fitting that today the interior of the mammoth papal palace in Avignon, a favorite tourist attraction, is bare.) After the fourteenth century the papacy, bereaved of its position as the spiritual, cultural, and political nucleus of the church universal, was but a pallid imitation of its famed

ancestor. The protestant reformation did not begin the
dissection of the church; the momentum towards universalism had been slowing down since 1300. In the
twentieth century the papacy enjoys the spiritual loyalty of but a fraction of the world's population. Modern
popes do not influence or participate in the decisions
made by national governments. One must go back to the
thirteenth century to find pontiffs who provided both
spiritual and political leadership on a world scale.

But the papacy contained a built-in contradiction.
Why did the Gregorian church fail? The main reasons
are two. First, the institution of the Gregorian papacy
outlived its social usefulness, as all institutions eventually do. From 1050 to 1250 the papal monarchy was
as successful as any institution could hope to be. Excel-
lent leaders, the popes during this period were in the
vanguard of progressive reform. The rapid economic up-
swing after 1050 induced a vague yearning for unity of
some kind. An unstable and anarchic Europe called
upon the popes to offer guidance and an ideal which
transcended sectional interests. The papacy became the
single most effective force for order, cooperation, peace,
reason, social justice.

But the papacy contained a built-in contradiction.
For while Christians wanted their popes to afford spiritual direction, they expected popes at the same time to
administer earthly justice. Both laymen and clerics took
their complaints to Rome in the hope of getting favorable judgments. And as the popes fought to maintain
their spiritual independence by preserving the Papal
States, they encountered the Hohenstaufen emperors.
Hence to meet both the demands of lawsuits appealed
to Rome and the need to cast off the Hohenstaufen
yoke, the pontiffs had to expand their judicial and administrative organization. The result was that by 1250
the organization had become so huge and unwieldy that
the running of it demanded a pope's total energy. The
institution took on a life of its own; it forgot about the
ends for which it was created. This self-protective bureau-

cracy in effect reduced a pope's options. Literally thousands of people throughout Europe had a stake in perpetuating the system. As political, socioeconomic, and cultural conditions in Europe changed, the papacy lagged behind and became isolated from the mainstream of developments. The curial organization was geared to centralize ever more power in the person of the pope who was not disposed to surrender any of this power. While Europe in 1150 may have needed a more unified church, in 1300 it needed a more regionalized church—but the machine would not slow down. Europe required a stimulus to local initiative, not more bureaucracy. People after 1250 were losing faith in the papacy because they naively expected it to do everything. They wanted a St Bernard and an Innocent III rolled into one. They were unaware that the papacy's inherent contradiction between prophecy and statemanship was no longer the creative force it once was—in 1300 the inconsistency was ripping the church apart.

Second, the Gregorian church failed because it could not adapt to the new political entity, the national secular state. The Gregorian papacy originated at a time when the West was politically fragmented into tiny units. A man's loyalty then was primarily to his family, lord, locality, and church. By the late thirteenth century, however, the secular state—especially in France, England, Spain—was assuming functions formerly carried out by the church. Unable to remake its structure vis-à-vis the rising monarchies, the papacy fought a holding action and retrenched behind its tradition.

In warding off Hohenstaufen advances, the papacy was compelled to rely on French aid, thereby effecting a perilous dependency on the Capetian monarchy. Papal political strategy unwittingly made French subjects more subservient, spiritually and materially, to the crown. The pope made it easier for the king to divide and subdue the various groups in the French realm. The pontiff's unpopular tactics in France made him a common object of enmity—utilized by the king to his own profit. Hence when the papal watchdog, the French king, turned on its master in Rome, the latter was defenseless. Intolerant of outside intrusions in his domestic affairs Philip the Fair annihilated Boniface VIII—and the papal monarchy.

The Gregorian church did not collapse because of bad popes. Man-made institutions (the historian, who can only describe human phenomena, will not object if the theologian insists on the church's divine origin) are not eternal. Europe permitted and even encouraged the realization of Gregory VII's dream. But by 1300 the implementation of the dream became an obstruction to new definitions of progress. Hence the Gregorian ideal was discarded.

BIRTH OF THE NATIONAL STATE

In France the new ideal emanating from Paris was national monarchy. In one sense, the crown exploited a latent national feeling already present in the realm; the campaign against Boniface VIII could never have succeeded without this embryonic attitude. In another, the government *created* national sentiment. It tried to convince the people that this sentiment was properly expressed in loyalty to the king. The Philip IV-Boniface VIII controversy was one of the reasons why the state in France preceded the nation. In Italy and Germany it was the opposite: the sense of common nationality preceded the state—both nations were not politically unified until the nineteenth century. But the strong political, administrative, and financial institutions built by St Louis and Philip the Fair gave the monarchy the relative power to impose a primitive form of nationalism on its people.

It must be admitted that by twentieth-century norms the French government's power was paltry indeed. Most Frenchmen only dimly recognized the public authority of the monarch. The king had no secret police, no standing army, no effective tax-gathering service. He was not expected to make laws (although in practice he occasionally did) but only protect local customs. He had to negotiate personally with individuals and groups concerning the amount of tax to be paid. Even after 1303 Philip never collected as much revenue from the clergy (or from the towns) as he needed for his wars. His actual power derived largely from his status as feudal overlord and as supreme judge.

But Philip the Fair scored an important victory for the monarchy: the acceptance of the principle of emergency powers. When the king decided that the country was in danger from external attack he could require monetary or military aid from all subjects in the realm. Already the king could be heard to accuse persons of "treason" (i.e., danger from internal attack) against himself and the nation. The idea of the nation state was not the brain child of the intelligentsia; it was a product of war. Philip equated national interest with his aggressive military action. The government shrouded his wars in religious symbolism. The king became God's vicar. The mystical body of the church somehow became the mystical body politic of the nation. France and the French people enjoyed God's special favor. The French soldier in Flanders became a crusader, and a sort of priest. Palestine, the traditional holy land, was becoming replaced by the new Holy Land, France. The king's flag, the oriflamme, became the herald of the Lord. Nobles, clergy, bourgeois—privileged groups whose traditional ethic was individualistic—were vehemently told that their freedom from taxation was treasonous and sinful.

France was the new universalist empire which would replace the former empires, the papacy and the Holy Roman Empire. In an effort to obtain a position at the royal court, Pierre Dubois, a Norman lawyer, devised in 1306 a grandiose plan which would make the French king the ruler of the world. The scenario was for the

king to lead a crusade to the Holy Land, crown himself
Holy Roman Emperor, confiscate the Papal States, subdue the communes of Italy, and install pro-French
popes. Dubois also suggested that French troops wear
uniforms and march to martial music. While Philip the
Fair never acted upon this fantastic scheme the dream
of a vast French empire was indeed entertained by the
more enthusiastic of his royal agents. Dubois articulated
their aspirations. Perhaps Europe was still too wedded
to the concept of a universal Christendom to conceive
of Europe without a common head, a common loyalty.
The particularist nation state, which generates its own
morality, borrowed its ideology and its methods from
the church and the Holy Roman Empire.

CONCLUSION

The ideal of a united Christendom faded in the fourteenth century. The papacy, the symbolic and organizational center of this unity, was unable to find enough
support for its claims to temporal and spiritual leadership.

With Philip the Fair France was clearly the superior
political might in the West. The universalist papacy
helped to destroy the Holy Roman Empire; France
destroyed the papacy.

The kingdom of France emerged as a nascent nation
state. The second revolution had begun. The first revolution—started by Gregory VII—had been superceded by
the rise of the secular national state. Within this new
form of community even the loyalty of the clergy was
directed to the king and the kingdom. The universalist
dream of a single Europe was being fragmented into an
aggregate of autonomous and particularist powers. The
Catholic church would be no longer catholic, for each
state would absorb its own church into the body politic.
Nationalism not universalism would herald a new
Europe.

Conclusion

Pope Gregory VII started the first revolution in medieval church-state relations. He proposed that the papacy serve not only as a symbol of Christian unity, but also as the impelling force which would organize the clergy into a separate class. Centered in Rome the clergy would ensure that Christian principles would govern all social relationships. The obstacle to Gregory's dream of a universal Christendom patterned after the makeup of heaven was the Holy Roman Emperor, the papacy's traditional ally, who also claimed universal authority and the right to control of the church. As it happened, the papacy eventually freed itself from German domination.

St Bernard of Clairvaux and Abelard accepted the basic design of the Gregorian church as did many other churchmen in the twelfth century. Although mavericks in other ways, these two monks did not challenge the existing episcopal structure and the pope's supremacy. But they insisted that an elite within the church should bear witness to the apostolic life as a corrective to the growing legalism within ecclesiastical organizations. For Bernard, this special group was his own Cistercian order of monks vowed to poverty, obedience, and isolation from society; these contemplatives were the reverse side of the rural lay aristocracy in France. For Abelard, the purifiers were the teachers of philosophy and theology

in the new urban schools; these activists would bring
Christians to God through reason and the new learning.
But in the end the quest of Bernard and Abelard for a
prophetic alternative only served to consolidate the
papal monarchy.

In the early thirteenth century St Francis of Assisi's
more flexible brand of charisma had much less to do
with the organizational church. Francis' happy wan-
derers needed only the witness of their lives to convert
the urban poor, a class often neglected by the clergy.
But Pope Innocent III, who sought to make the papacy
play a major role in ecclesiastical and secular affairs
throughout Europe, brought the Franciscan ideal of absolute poverty into the institutional church. Against
Francis' wishes, Franciscans took their place in the
ranks of the papal army. Innocent's successors tried to
use the mendicants to strengthen the papacy's hold over
the church and to drive the German emperor out of
Italy.

The papacy's willingness to use fully its spiritual
weapons against the emperors, especially Frederick II of
Hohenstaufen, weakened its prestige and made it dependent on France. The papal attack on the Hohenstaufen
hastened the decentralization of Germany and the triumph of the German princes. The French king, St
Louis, came to fulfill the universalist role vacated by
both pope and emperor. Louis not only bolstered the
position of the monarchy in France and in Europe, he
gave secular kingship a religious quality. His authority to
rule was believed to come directly from God, bypassing
the intermediary of the church.

Philip the Fair's victory over Pope Boniface VIII shattered forever the Gregorian ideal of a united Christendom. By Philip's death in 1314 France was clearly the
dominant power in the West. The *first* revolution in-
augurated the movement towards European unity under
the papacy; Christian society was ideally subdivided into
priests and laymen. With the *second* revolution the

secular state sought to merge clergy and laity into a single body politic. A national church was absorbed into the nation state, the new political ideal. Church-state conflicts within the national state would presumably not occur because the king, the embodiment of the nation, demanded the absolute loyalty of all subjects. After the divination of the French people and the territory of France, there was no further need for a universal Christian society.

The period of European history 1050-1300, which witnessed the rise and decline of the universal papacy, can be suitably labeled the high middle ages. This era marks the peak of medieval civilization, the period of its most spectacular achievements. This is not to suggest that the popes were the primary cause of the economic, cultural, and institutional developments during these centuries. The activities of popes were far from the minds of most Europeans; the Gregorian ideal in fact never came even close to becoming actualized. Yet the papal movement was the single most dynamic source of inspiration to constructive action. This civilizing process worked towards the creation of new forms of cooperative efforts and material progress. The holy see provided a skeleton around which the body of "Europe" could grow. The papacy fired up enthusiasm among Europeans and exhorted them to organize society along Christian lines—in a union of spiritual and temporal. The pontiffs replaced the otherworldly ethos of monasticism with an ethic which could adapt to and change an urban-commercial society.

When this universal ideal failed, the unity implicit in medieval culture disintegrated. During the confusion of the fourteenth and fifteenth centuries Europeans looked for political ideals which would replace the old universalism. Many forsook ecclesiastical structures and experimented with unorthodox forms of religion. By the sixteenth century it was clear that the national state would furnish the framework for cultural and institutional evolution.

The religious divisions which resulted from the Reformation hastened the development towards separate states within Europe. Even more detrimental to any prospect of European unity was the fervent nationalism which affected European countries in the nineteenth century. The experience of two world wars in the twentieth century has further diminished chances for a restored European community.

Yet despite these ideological, political, and institutional tendencies towards autonomous states, it remains true that Europeans have never in any period since the middle ages completely lost their sense of cultural uniqueness. Children of the medieval Gregorian era, they have continued to be convinced of their superiority and their special world mission—a mission which transcends national identity. A resurgence of this latent Europeanism followed World War II, at which time Europeans found themselves wedged between two superpowers. Since 1945 many Europeans have expressed a desire for some kind of political unification, which might even necessitate the partial abandonment of national sovereignty.

It is widely held in Europe and America that society can and should be consciously structured according to a priori principles. By sheer force of will and by the law, it is said, the social order can be refashioned to conform to rational patterns. In the middle ages the ultimate pattern was the "right order" (modeled after heaven) pursued by the Gregorian popes; the clergy had the right and the capacity to Christianize the whole of society. In the modern world the models are more subjective and secular. Appealing to no law above itself, the modern state presumes to nationalize its citizenry according to any paradigm which seems feasible at any given moment. The West seems as yet unwilling to abandon this aspect of its medieval heritage.

HOLY ROMAN EMPIRE AT THE TIME OF FREDERICK II OF HOHENSTAUFEN

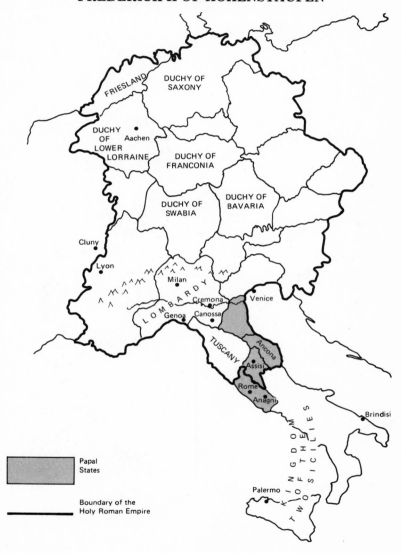

FRANCE IN 1260

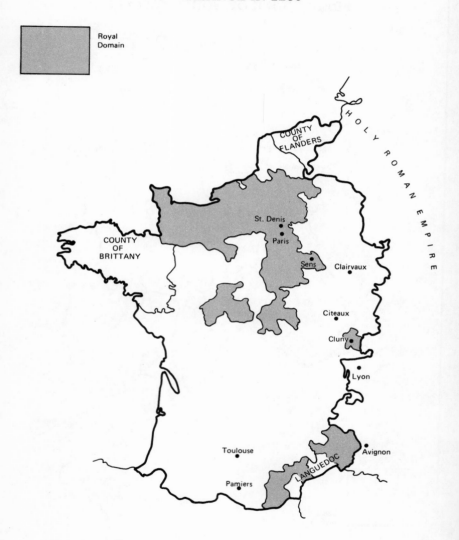

Royal Domain

COUNTY OF FLANDERS

HOLY ROMAN EMPIRE

COUNTY OF BRITTANY

St. Denis

Paris

Sens

Clairvaux

Citeaux

Cluny

Lyon

Toulouse

Avignon

LANGUEDOC

Pamiers

Dates

1056-1106 King Henry IV (Emperor after 1084)

1059 Papal election decree

1073-1085 Gregory VII's pontificate

1075 *Dictatus Papae*
Gregory VII outlaws lay investiture

1076 Gregory VII excommunicates and deposes Henry IV

1077 Canossa
German princes elect antiking Rudolf (d. 1080)

1080 Gregory VII again excommunicates and deposes Henry IV

1084 Henry IV crowned emperor in Rome by his antipope Clement
Normans sack Rome
Gregory VII flees to Sicily

1089-1099 Urban II's pontificate

1095-1099 First Crusade

1079-1142 Peter Abelard

1090-1153 St Bernard of Clairvaux

1098 Robert of Molesme founds Citeaux: beginning of Cistercian order

1112 Bernard enters Citeaux

1115 Bernard founds Clairvaux

c.1119 Separation of Heloise and Abelard

1121 Synod at Soissons condemns Abelard

1122 Concordat of Worms settles investiture controversy

1130-1137 Papal schism: Innocent II vs. Anaclet

c.1135 Abelard resumes teaching in Paris

c.1139 William of St Thierry writes to Bernard

1140 Council of Sens condemns Abelard

1181?-1226 St Francis of Assisi

1190-1197 Emperor Henry VI

1194-1250 Frederick II, son of Henry VI

1198-1216 Innocent III's pontificate

1198 Philip of Swabia elected King of the Romans by German princes
Otto of Brunswick elected antiking

1201-1204 Fourth crusade

1206 Conversion of St Francis

1208 Frederick becomes king of Sicily

1209 Start of "crusade" against Cathars in southern France

1210 Innocent III gives verbal approval of St Francis' rule

1211 Frederick elected king of Germany

1214 Bouvines: French defeat Otto and the English

1215 Frederick crowned at Aachen
Lateran council

1220 Frederick elected Emperor of the Romans in Rome and returns to Sicily. His son Henry elected king of the Romans and goes to Germany
Frederick grants concessions to German prince-bishops

1220-1225 Frederick subdues Sicily

1223 St Francis' 2nd Rule

1226-1234 Barons rebel against Louis IX and Blanche

1226-1270 Reign of St Louis IX of France

1227-1241 Gregory IX's pontificate

1227 Gregory IX excommunicates Frederick

1227-1229 Crusade of Frederick

1230 Peace between Frederick and Gregory IX

1236-1239 Frederick's invasions of Lombardy

1243-1254 Innocent IV's pontificate

1245 At Lyon Innocent IV excommunicates and deposes Frederick

1248-1254 First crusade of Louis IX

Suggested Readings

GENERAL

Barraclough, G., *The Medieval Papacy*, New York, 1968.

——, *The Origins of Modern Germany*, New York, 1947.

Cambridge Medieval History, vols. 5, 6, 7, London, 1926-32.

Hill, B.D., ed., *Church and State in the Middle Ages*, New York, 1970.

McIlwain, C.H., *The Growth of Political Thought in the West*, New York, 1932.

Morrall, J.B., *Political Thought in Medieval Times*, New York, 1962.

Southern, R.W., *The Making of the Middle Ages*, New Haven, 1961.

Sturzo, L., *Church and State*, vol. 1, Notre Dame, 1962.

Tierney, B., *The Crisis of Church and State, 1050-1300*, Englewood Cliffs, N.J., 1964.

Ullmann, W., *The Growth of Papal Government in the Middle Ages*, 3rd ed., London, 1970.

——, *A Short History of the Papacy in the Middle Ages*, London, 1972.

GREGORY VII AND HENRY IV

Benson, R.L., ed., intro. by K.F. Morrison, *Imperial Lives and Letters of the Eleventh Century*, New York, 1962.

Emerton, E., ed., *The Correspondence of Pope Gregory VII*, New York, 1969.

Morrison, K.F., ed., *The Investiture Controversy: Issues, Ideals, and Results*, New York, 1971.

Tellenbach, G., *Church, State, and Christian Society at the Time of the Investiture Contest*, New York, 1970.

Tierney, B., and others, eds., *Gregory VII—Church Reformer or World Monarch?*, New York, 1967.

Williams, S., ed., *The Gregorian Epoch: Reformation, Revolution, Reaction?*, Boston, 1964.

ABELARD AND ST BERNARD OF CLAIRVAUX

Abelard, *Historia Calamitatum*, trans. J.T. Muckle as *The Story of Abelard's Adversities*, Toronto, 1964.

——, *Ethics*, trans. D.E. Luscombe, Oxford, 1971.

Bernard of Clairvaux, *Letters*, trans. B.S. James, Chicago, 1953.

——, *On the Song of Songs*, trans. K. Walsh, Spencer, Mass., 1971.

Grane, L., *Peter Abelard*, New York, 1970.

Leclercq, J., "Saint Bernard on the Church," *Downside Review*, 85(1967) pp.274-94.

Murray, A.V., *Abelard and St. Bernard: A Study in Twelfth Century "Modernism,"* New York, 1967.

Sikes, J.G., *Peter Abailard*, New York 1965, orig. 1932.

White, H.V., "The Gregorian Ideal and St. Bernard of Clairvaux," *Journal of the History of Ideas*, 21(1960) pp.321-48.

ST FRANCIS AND INNOCENT III

Cheney, C.R., and Semple, W.H., eds., *Selected Letters of Pope Innocent III concerning England*, Edinburgh, 1953.

Elliott-Binns, L., *Innocent III*, Hamden, Conn., 1968, orig. 1931.

Francis of Assisi, trans. B. Fahy as *The Writings of St Francis of Assisi*, Chicago, 1964.

Hughes, S., trans. *The Little Flowers of St. Francis and Other Franciscan Writings*, New York, 1964.

Lambert, M.D., *Franciscan Poverty*, London, 1961.

Packard, S.R., *Europe and the Church under Innocent III*, New York, 1968, orig. 1927.

Powell, J.M., ed., *Innocent III: Vicar of Christ or Lord of the World?*, Boston, 1963.

Smith, J.H., *Francis of Assisi*, New York, 1972.

Strayer, J.R., *The Albigensian Crusades*, New York, 1971.

Thomas of Celano, *Saint Francis of Assisi*, trans. P. Hermann, Chicago, 1963.

FREDERICK II AND ST LOUIS

Andrewes, P., *Frederick II of Hohenstaufen*, London, 1970.

Joinville, *The Life of St. Louis* in *Chronicles of the Crusades*, trans. M.R.B. Shaw, Baltimore, 1963.

Kantorowicz, E., *Frederick the Second, 1194-1250*, London, 1957, orig. in German 1931.

Labarge, M.W., *Saint Louis*, Boston, 1968.

Powell, J.M., trans. *The Liber Augustalis*, Syracuse, 1971.

Van Cleve, T.C., *The Emperor Frederick II of Hohenstaufen*, Oxford, 1972.

PHILIP THE FAIR AND BONIFACE VIII

Boase, T.S.R., *Boniface VIII*, London, 1933.

Dubois, Pierre, *The Recovery of the Holy Land*, trans. W.I. Brandt, New York, 1956.

Ergang, R., *Emergence of the National State*, New York, 1971.

Strayer, J.R., "Consent to Taxation under Philip the Fair" in Strayer and C.H. Taylor, *Studies in Early French Taxation,,* Cambridge, Mass., 1939.

——, *Medieval Statecraft and the Perspectives of History* (essays), Princeton, 1971.

Wood, C.T., ed., *Philip the Fair and Boniface VIII*, 2nd ed., New York, 1971.